THE LINDBERGH BABY KIDNAPPING TRIAL

A Headline Court Case

Headline Court Cases

The Andersonville Prison Civil War Crimes Trial
A Headline Court Case
0-7660-1386-3

The John Brown Slavery Revolt Trial
A Headline Court Case
0-7660-1385-5

The Lindbergh Baby Kidnapping Trial
A Headline Court Case
0-7660-1389-8

The Lizzie Borden "Axe Murder" Trial
A Headline Court Case
0-7660-1422-3

The Nuremberg Nazi War Crimes Trials
A Headline Court Case
0-7660-1384-7

The Sacco and Vanzetti Controversial Murder Trial
A Headline Court Case
0-7660-1387-1

The Salem Witchcraft Trials
A Headline Court Case
0-7660-1383-9

The Scopes Monkey Trial
A Headline Court Case
0-7660-1388-X

THE LINDBERGH BABY KIDNAPPING TRIAL

A Headline Court Case

Judy Monroe

Enslow Publishers, Inc.

40 Industrial Road   PO Box 38
Box 398   Aldershot
Berkeley Heights, NJ 07922   Hants GU12 6BP
USA   UK

http://www.enslow.com

Library of Congress Cataloging-in-Publication Data

Monroe, Judy.
 The Lindbergh baby kidnapping trial: a headline court case/ Judy
Monroe.
   p. cm. — (Headline court cases)
 Includes bibliographical references and index.
 Summary: Presents information about the kidnapping of Charles
Lindbergh's baby in 1932, the investigation of the crime, and the
subsequent trial of Bruno Hauptmann; includes commentary on the
decision.
  ISBN 0-7660-1389-8
  1. Lindbergh, Charles A. (Charles Augustus), 1902–1974—Trials,
litigation, etc.—Juvenile literature. 2. Hauptmann, Bruno Richard,
1899–1936—Trials, litigation, etc.—Juvenile literature. 3. Lindbergh,
Charles Augustus, 1930–1932—Kidnapping, 1932—Juvenile literature.
4. Trials (Kidnapping)—New Jersey—Flemington—Juvenile literature.
5. Kidnapping—New Jersey—Hopewell—Juvenile literature. [1. Lindbergh,
Charles A. (Charles Augustus), 1902-1974—Trials, litigation, etc.
2. Hauptmann, Bruno Richard, 1899–1936—Trials, litigation, etc.
3. Lindbergh, Charles Augustus, 1930–1932—Kidnapping, 1932. 4. Trials
(Kidnapping) 5. Kidnapping.] I. Title. II. Series.
   KF223.L53 M66 2000
   345.73'0254—dc21
                                                       99-050666

Printed in the United States of America

10 9 8 7 6 5 4 3 2 1

To Our Readers:
All Internet addresses in this book were active and appropriate when we went to press.
Any comments or suggestions can be sent by e-mail to Comments@enslow.com or to
the address on the back cover.

Photo Credits: New Jersey State Police Museum Archives, pp. 32, 41, 59, 66,
71, 78, 83, 86, 96; Prints and Photographs Division, Library of Congress, pp. 3,
8, 17, 19, 27, 36, 51, 62, 90, 106, 112.

Cover Photo: Prints and Photographs Division, Library of Congress

Contents

chapter one

STOLEN BABY

HOPEWELL, NJ—Despite a cold, twenty-month-old Charles Lindbergh, Jr., nicknamed Charlie, had finally fallen asleep. His mother, Anne Morrow Lindbergh, and nurse, Betty Gow, latched two of the three sets of window shutters in the nursery. But the shutters at the corner window were warped and the two women pulling together could not close and latch them, so they were left unlatched. Anne Lindbergh left the nursery about 7:30 that Tuesday evening, March 1, 1932. Betty Gow stayed behind to do some small tasks, leaving the nursery at about 7:50 P.M. She then went to help with some sewing.

At about 8:25 P.M., Colonel Charles Lindbergh arrived home. The Lindberghs ate their evening meal and soon afterward went into the living room. About a half-hour later, Colonel Lindbergh heard an odd noise. He told his wife, "I thought I heard a sound like breaking wood."[1] No one investigated, however.

By 10:00 P.M., the colonel had settled into the library downstairs. Mrs. Lindbergh was upstairs taking a bath. Betty Gow went to check on little Charlie. As soon as she walked into the nursery, she plugged in an electric heater to ward off the chill in the room. A late-winter rainstorm was raging outside the newly finished house, located in a remote rural area of Hopewell, New Jersey.

Gow walked toward the crib, but could not hear the baby breathing. Placing her hand on the crib's railing, she looked into the crib. The baby was missing. She searched through the baby's blankets, but could not find Charlie.

Gow ran from the nursery to the Lindberghs' bedroom, where Mrs. Lindbergh had settled for the night, to ask if she

Charlie Lindbergh was kidnapped from this crib on March 1, 1932.

had the baby. When she said no, Gow rushed downstairs to the library, located one floor below the nursery. Bursting into the room, Gow asked the colonel if he had the baby. Shaking his head no, Lindbergh rose from behind his desk. He sprinted upstairs to the nursery, with Gow close behind him. Lindbergh quickly looked into the crib, then marched into the master bedroom. He took a rifle from the closet and loaded it. Carrying the loaded rifle, he returned to the nursery, followed by the two women. The colonel faced his wife and said, "Anne, they have stolen our baby."[2]

Lindbergh then instructed the caretaker of the house to call the local police. After that call was made, the colonel made two telephone calls. The first was to the family lawyer, who was also a personal friend. Lindbergh's second call was to the New Jersey State Police.

Within hours of the telephone calls, newspaper reporters began arriving at the Lindberghs' home. They had many questions: Who had taken the Lindbergh baby? What did the kidnappers want from the Lindberghs? Had the kidnappers left any clues? And where was little Charlie?

chapter two

AMERICA IN THE 1930s

AMERICA—The year of little Charlie Lindbergh's kidnapping was 1932. At that time, America was undergoing major political and economic changes. Some of these upheavals and issues would have an effect on the Lindbergh baby kidnapping case.

Prohibition

One controversial issue of this period was Prohibition. The movement to prohibit, or stop, the manufacture and sale of alcoholic beverages in America began in the early 1800s. Pressure from this movement grew over the decades. Finally, in January 1919, both the House of Representatives and the Senate passed the Eighteenth Amendment to the Constitution of the United States. This law said that no alcohol could be manufactured, imported, exported, transported, or sold in the United States.

To get around the law, some Americans turned to illegal activities. They went to places called speakeasies where alcoholic beverages were sold illegally. People also made, sold, and transported their own illegal beers, wines, and other alcoholic beverages. Moonshining—the making of home-made whiskey—and smuggling greatly increased during Prohibition. Al Capone (1899–1947) was known as the King of Bootleg Liquor, that is, illegally made alcohol. During the 1920s, he ruled Chicago's crime world and made huge sums of money from his illegal liquor sales. He was finally jailed in 1931 for not paying his taxes.

Because of all this illegal alcohol activity, the number of violent crimes skyrocketed. For example, within a few years of the passage of the Eighteenth Amendment (in 1919), the prison population increased greatly. Because of the increase in crime and violence, people began to ask that the law against alcohol be reversed. (It was eventually reversed in 1933.)

The Crash of 1929

While the battle over Prohibition was raging and violent crimes were occurring more frequently, many Americans became part of an event that shook the very economic foundations of the nation—the stock market crash of 1929.

Following the end of World War I (1914–1918), the United States had entered a period of slow economic growth. By the time Herbert Hoover became the thirty-first American president in 1929, the country had moved into a period of great prosperity. Many people were earning high wages. In turn, they had more money to spend and invest in the stock market.

During the first six months of Hoover's presidency,

stock prices reached new heights. They reached their all-time high on September 3, 1929. By this time, people across the country had invested billions of dollars in the stock market. But by October 1929, the buying frenzy came to an abrupt halt, and turned into a frantic wave of stock selling. As a result, stock prices plunged. Thousands of people lost all they had invested, and faced complete financial ruin.

On October 29, 1929, seven months after Hoover had taken office, the New York Stock Exchange, the largest in the world, had its worst day of panic selling. One New York Stock Exchange guard said that the people there "hollered and screamed, they clawed at one another's collars. It was like a bunch of crazy men."[1] What would this economic crash mean to America and the world?

The Great Depression

The answer came quickly. Within six months, 4 million Americans had lost their jobs and by the end of 1931, that number had soared to 13.5 million.[2] The crash of the American stock market preceded economic hard times, known as the Great Depression. The depression spread across the United States, and almost every country in the world by the early 1930s.

In the United States, many factories closed, unemployment increased, and banks failed in growing numbers. The price of things like food, metals, oil, and lumber fell steadily. By 1932, thousands of banks had failed, hundreds of mills and factories had closed, and many people had lost their farms, businesses, and homes. For those who still had jobs, their pay often dropped by as much as half, and sometimes more.

The 1932 American presidential campaign focused on the issues of Prohibition and the economic crisis. Franklin Delano Roosevelt, the Democratic candidate for president, called for a repeal, or reversal, of the Eighteenth Amendment. He also promised big changes in economic and social matters so that America would recover from the Great Depression. Roosevelt won the election and went on to become the thirty-second president of the United States.

Kidnapping Epidemic

In addition to Prohibition and the Great Depression, America faced another crisis—a kidnapping epidemic. A sudden increase in kidnappings was seen across the country. The kidnappings were usually committed by gangsters and members of organized gangs. Adults were generally the ones being kidnapped, sometimes as a result of power wars between rival groups or fights over illegal alcohol deals.

By the early 1930s, kidnappings had become big business. They were occurring in many places across the country. In 1932, the year little Charlie Lindbergh was abducted, kidnappings had spread from gang members to wealthy families and the general public, including children. Because of kidnappings, said historian Paula S. Fass, "Americans had become helpless victims of gangland crime. Kidnapping was seen by the press and public as an important symbol for the general lawlessness that seemed to be swirling across the country."[3]

Although kidnappings and violent crimes had become common and people were feeling the effects of the Great Depression, Charlie Lindbergh's abduction made front page news in America and in many countries around the world. Hoards of local and state police, reporters, and curious people came to the Lindberghs' home soon after the kidnapping was reported. Why was baby Charlie's kidnapping so newsworthy?

The Lindberghs

Charles Augustus Lindbergh, Jr., was born on June 22, 1930, at the beginning of the Great Depression. His parents, Charles Augustus Lindbergh and Anne Morrow Lindbergh, were young, attractive, rich, and very famous.

Charles Augustus Lindbergh. The baby's father, Charles Augustus Lindbergh, was born in the small town of Little Falls, Minnesota, on February 4, 1902. At age eighteen he went to the University of Wisconsin, but dropped out after two years to go to flying school. Seven months later, Lindbergh was a pilot. To earn money, he took various piloting jobs and flew the mail between Saint Louis, Missouri, and Chicago, Illinois.

At this time, the field of aviation, or flying, was still young. It was only in 1903 that Orville and Wilbur Wright, two American brothers, had made the world's first airplane flight. In 1925, a New York hotel owner named Raymond Orteig offered twenty-five thousand dollars to the first person who could fly solo, nonstop, across the Atlantic Ocean. The flight would start in New York and end in France, thirty-six hundred miles away. The prize went unclaimed for over a year.

Now Charles Lindbergh, age twenty-five, climbed into his small, noisy monoplane (one engine), which he had named *Spirit of St. Louis*, to attempt to cross the Atlantic Ocean. The only extra items he had packed were five sandwiches and some water. Lindbergh used a new type of compass to help him maintain a straight course through bad weather. However, he had no radio and used primitive tools—such as the stars and a folding map—to guide his flight. Lindbergh took off from Long Island, New York, on May 20, 1927.

Radio stations, the transatlantic cable, and newspapers around the world tracked Lindbergh's flight. The media were calling him *Lucky Lindy* and the *Flying Fool*. After thirty-three hours and twenty-nine minutes, Lindbergh circled the Eiffel Tower in Paris, France, then landed. He was greeted by an excited, cheering crowd of one hundred thousand people.[4] The flight made Lindbergh an instant hero, especially in the United States and Europe.

When he returned to the United States, 4 million people honored Lindbergh with a ticker tape parade in New York City. This was the biggest parade New York had ever seen. As a result of his successful flight, Lindbergh was commissioned a colonel in the United States Air Service Reserve and became a technical adviser to commercial airlines. Meanwhile, Congress voted to create the Distinguished Flying Cross medal, which was awarded to Lindbergh. The

Charles A. Lindbergh made history with his 1927 flight across the Atlantic Ocean. His plane, the Spirit of St. Louis, *is behind him.*

Post Office issued a new airmail stamp in Lindbergh's honor. And *Time* magazine made him its first Man of the Year. Across the nation, thousands danced to the Lindy Hop and the radio featured songs and marches created for the hero now called the Lone Eagle.

Anne Spencer Morrow Lindbergh. Born on June 22, 1907, Anne Spencer Morrow's father, Dwight Morrow (1873–1931), was an American ambassador and influential banker. She was a millionaire heiress. Already showing talent as a writer, the petite, shy young woman had published stories and poems in her college's magazine. During her senior year at Smith College in Northampton, Massachusetts, she won both of the school's top literary prizes. Soon after Charles Lindbergh's historic flight, Anne Morrow's father invited Lindbergh to the Morrows' home, where Lindbergh met the Morrow family—including Anne. After meeting Charles Lindbergh, twenty-one-year-old Anne Morrow developed a crush, calling him "the last of the gods."[5]

During fall 1928, Lindbergh dated Morrow. Sometimes he gave her flying lessons. The two became engaged, and then married on May 27, 1929.

In March 1930, a pregnant Anne Lindbergh earned her pilot's license and became the colonel's radio operator, copilot, and navigator on many air journeys. In April 1930, Charles and Anne Lindbergh broke the transcontinental (across the continent) speed record, flying from Los Angeles to New York in fourteen hours and forty-five minutes. The couple became known as the "first romancers of the air."[6]

Anne Morrow married Charles Lindbergh on May 27, 1929. After the marriage, she became Colonel Lindbergh's radio operator, copilot, and navigator on many flights.

Although they seldom gave interviews, Charles and Anne Lindbergh were constantly hounded by the press. Wherever they went, someone would soon spot them, and they would be mobbed by admirers and reporters. So, the Lindberghs sometimes used disguises and gave fake names to pass unnoticed.

On June 22, 1928, her twenty-fourth birthday, Anne Morrow Lindbergh gave birth to Charles Augustus Lindbergh, Jr. The front pages of newspapers told Americans the good news. Because Lindbergh was known as the Lone Eagle, the press began calling the baby the Eaglet. When Charlie was about a year old, he was left with Anne Lindbergh's parents while the Lindberghs made an air survey of the Far East, to find a route for air travel from the United States to China. The trip was cut short in October 1931 when Dwight Morrow, Anne Lindbergh's father, died.

After the Lindberghs returned to the United States, the press and admirers continued to pursue them. To gain some privacy, the couple moved from Anne Morrow's parents' home in Englewood, New Jersey, to a fourteen-room house they built on four hundred acres of land near Hopewell, a rural area of New Jersey. After the press ran articles and photos of the house, many sightseers came to look at the Lindberghs' house.

It was a two-hour drive to New York City from the house. Once the house was nearly finished, the family stayed there from Saturday through Monday morning. Then Charles Lindbergh would go to his job in New York City with Trans-Continental Air Transport. During the week, the couple stayed at the Morrow mansion in Englewood, New Jersey.

This regular routine was changed on Monday, February 29, 1932. At that time, Anne Lindbergh was three months' pregnant with her second child, Jon, and both she and baby Charlie had colds. The Lindberghs stayed at their new home in Hopewell that Monday and the next evening. It was on Tuesday, March 2, 1932, wrote Charles Lindbergh in his autobiography, that "a tragedy took place that was to affect our lives forever. Our son, Charles, Jr., was kidnapped. . . . He was twenty months old, blond, blue-eyed, and just beginning to talk."[7] The press called the Lindbergh baby kidnapping the Crime of the Century.

chapter three

THE ROAD TO COURT

BRONX—The Lindberghs and the police immediately began searching for the missing baby. As the search dragged on, Colonel Charles Lindbergh took charge of the investigation. Finally, in the fall of 1934, almost two years after the kidnapping, the New Jersey State Police informed the Lindberghs that they had caught the kidnapper. The accused kidnapper, Bruno Richard Hauptmann, was a carpenter.

The Initial Crime Scene

After nurse Betty Gow alerted the Lindberghs that Charlie was missing, the colonel "went upstairs to the child's nursery, opened the door, and immediately noticed a lifted window. A strange-looking envelope lay on the sill."[1] He told everyone not to touch the white envelope (so that the police could check it for any fingerprints). Then, with his rifle in hand, Lindbergh went outside to search for the kidnappers. He first went to the nursery end of the house and there saw a broken ladder. According to Lindbergh, the ladder "obviously had collapsed as the kidnapper descended. It looked as though it had been made out of new crating boards."[2]

Colonel Lindbergh returned to his house and called the state police. Then the "New Jersey State Police headquarters sent out a general alarm. Roadblocks were established, cars searched, neighbors awakened and questioned. Police officials assembled at our home. Carloads of reporters and photographers arrived" at the Lindbergh home.[3]

The local police arrived first. They and the colonel looked for clues in the nursery. They noticed clumps of soil on the baby's leather suitcase that lay beneath the open nursery window with the unlatched shutters. When they went outside, they found two indentations in the mud, probably impressions from where the ladder had stood. A set of footprints led from the house to a homemade wooden ladder, about seventy-five feet from the house. The ladder was in two sections, and the police concluded that it was the ladder that the kidnapper had used to get to the nursery window. About ten feet farther away, they found a third section of the ladder. No one touched the ladder. Everyone returned to the house to wait for the New Jersey State Police.

Several state police officers arrived just before eleven o'clock that stormy night. More arrived within an hour, including Colonel H. Norman Schwarzkopf, head of the New Jersey State Police. The police soon found a chisel in the mud below the nursery window. In their report, the police wrote that the kidnapper had brought the chisel to force open the nursery shutters, if necessary. No one, though, measured the footprints outside or made a cast of the shoe impressions, which might have helped the police in their investigation.

After the state police arrived, the ladder was inspected more closely. It had broken, possibly when the kidnapper had come down with the baby. The ladder weighed thirty-eight pounds, and although crudely made, it was well designed. Each section was narrower than the one below. The ladder fit into the two impressions left in the wet soil beneath the nursery window.

The nursery and envelope were dusted for fingerprints. Nothing was found except for a smudge on the envelope. Inside the envelope was a piece of paper. The police handed the paper, a ransom note, to Charles Lindbergh. The message was handwritten in blue ink, and the amount of money demanded was a good amount at this time:

> Dear Sir!
>
> Have 50,000$ redy [sic] 25,000$ in 20$ bills 15,000$ in 10$ bills and 10,000$ in 5$ bills. After 2–4 days we will inform you were to deliver the Mony [sic]. We warn you for making anyding [sic] public or for the polise [sic] the child is in gut [sic] care.
>
> Indication for all letters are signature and 3 holes.[4]

The indication was an unusual symbol on the bottom right-hand corner of the note. The symbol was of two interlocking circles. Each circle was a little larger than a quarter. Where the two circles overlapped was a solid red mark the size of a nickel. One small hole had been punched in the center of the red mark. The other two holes were in line with it but just outside the larger circles. Dusting the ransom note did not produce any fingerprints.

When the ladder was dusted for fingerprints, none showed up. Fingerprints did not appear on the chisel either. The kidnapper, reported the police in their write-up of the crime, probably wore gloves to avoid leaving fingerprints. The police concluded that the kidnapping had been well planned. The kidnappers must have studied the Lindbergh home's layout as well as the routine of the household.

At dawn the next morning, police began searching the surrounding grounds and woods. Scores of newspaper reporters, photographers, cameramen, and radio commentators continued to descend on the Lindbergh estate. So had more state police and curious people. Colonel Schwarzkopf, with hundreds of state troopers and police, finally secured the area, keeping the media to the far end of the grounds. However, any clues left by the kidnappers probably were destroyed by the many curiosity seekers and hundreds of reporters and photographers who had flocked to the Lindberghs' home.

The kidnapping made front-page news all over the world within a day. The leaders of Great Britain, France, Japan, and China, as well as President Herbert Hoover of the United States, and thousands of other people, sent letters, telegrams, and sympathy cards to the Lindberghs. Some of the letters, though, contained ransom demands, death threats, and psychic predictions.

Offers of help poured in. The Boy Scouts of America and students at nearby Princeton University offered to

the stairs, on the pantry sink. The telephone goes all day and night. People sleep all over the floors on newspapers and blankets."[6]

By the end of the first day, no one had found anything new. Nothing had been heard from the kidnappers. Colonel Lindbergh told Schwarzkopf that his first priority was getting Charlie back safely. This was more important than the arrest of the criminals.

Over the next few days, thousands of pieces of mail arrived at the Lindberghs' house. Three state police officers worked full-time to sort through the mail, looking for useful clues or information. As they considered the crime itself, the evidence, and the ransom note, the state police and Colonel Lindbergh developed three different theories about the kidnappers.

Person	The Kidnappers Were . . .
Colonel Charles Lindbergh	Professionals, perhaps gang members, given the fact that many kidnappings at that time were gang-related.
Colonel Schwarzkopf	Local and unprofessional, given the fact that the amount of ransom money demanded, while a lot for that time, was still rather low.
Lieutenant Keaton, Schwarzkopf's main detective	Members of the Lindbergh or Morrow staff, given the fact that they were probably the only ones who knew of the changes in the regular routine of the Lindberghs' living arrangements.

News from the Kidnappers

On March 4, the Lindberghs received a second ransom letter, mailed from Brooklyn, New York. Lindbergh and the police knew that this letter was from the kidnappers because of the unique symbol on the bottom right-hand corner—it was the same three interlocking holes and colors. There were similarities in the language and spelling. And, like the first ransom note, this one was handwritten:

> Dear Sir. We have warned you note [sic] to make anything public also notify the police now you have to take consequences—means we will have to hold the baby until everything is quiet. We can note [sic] make any appointment just now. . . . We are interested to send him back in gut [sic] health. And ransom was made aus [sic] for 50,000$ but now we have to take another person to it and probably have to keep the baby for a longer time as we expected. So the amount will be 70,000.[7]

A day later, another ransom letter arrived. It was basically a repeat of the letter of March 4. According to the terms of the ransom letter, Lindbergh and the police had to find a go-between, someone who would talk to the kidnappers, hand over the ransom money, and pick up little Charlie. One week after the kidnapping, Dr. John F. Condon offered to be the go-between. Through a series of letters and newspaper ads, Lindbergh, Condon, and the kidnappers agreed to this arrangement and a plan was developed.

Meeting with the Kidnappers

Seventy-one-year-old Dr. John (Jafsie) Francis Condon was a retired teacher, principal, and athletic coach. He and his wife lived in the Bronx, a borough of New York City. When he first read of the Lindbergh baby kidnapping, Condon was outraged over such a crime against America's great hero.[8] As a result of this outrage, he wrote a letter to the *Bronx Home News*, a local newspaper, offering to help deal with the kidnappers and act as a go-between, if needed. Over one hundred thousand people subscribed to this newspaper at this time.

The newspaper published Condon's letter on March 8, 1932. Condon had offered one thousand dollars of his own money to be added to the ransom money and said he would act as the go-between. The next day, he received a hand-written letter from the kidnapper. The kidnapper accepted him as a go-between and instructed him to put a message in the *New York American*, another newspaper, when the ransom money was ready.

Condon read the kidnapper's letter to Lindbergh over the telephone and then described the three interlocking circles at the bottom of the note. Lindbergh immediately met with Condon. Afterward, Condon placed the message in the *New York American*, as instructed. The kidnapper agreed to the plan of receiving the Lindberghs' money in exchange for the child.

In preparation, Colonel Lindbergh arranged with his bankers to bundle up seventy thousand dollars. The bank clerks used gold notes, or bills, for all of the ransom money. These bills had a round yellow seal on them, so they looked different from regular bills. In addition, the federal government was gradually withdrawing these notes from circulation. This fact made them rare and noticeable. The ransom money took eight hours to prepare for delivery, including the gathering, packaging, and recording of each gold note. The gold notes were also photographed. The serial number for each gold note was recorded, and later this list was distributed to thousands of banks across the country.

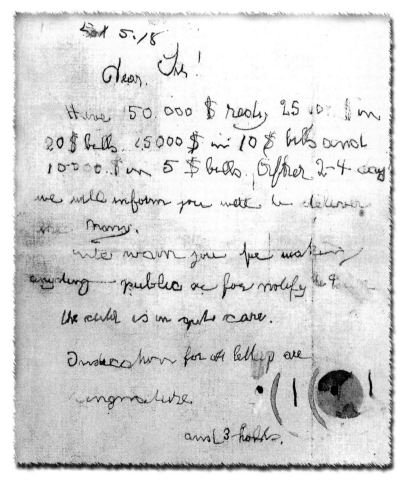

On the night of the kidnapping, the kidnapper left this ransom note in the baby's nursery.

The money was divided into two packages. One package contained the fifty thousand dollars that had been requested in the first ransom note. The other package contained an additional twenty thousand dollars, as requested in the second ransom note. Then through a combination of newspaper ads and mailed letters, Colonel Lindbergh, Condon, and the kidnapper agreed to meet on April 2, 1932, at night, on the edge of St. Raymond's Cemetery in the Bronx.

That night, Lindbergh drove Condon to the large cemetery across from the appointed area. No one else came with them. Lindbergh recalled,

> I parked across the street from the designated spot. The area was dimly lighted by city lamps. Soon a man appeared on the sidewalk next to the cemetery. . . . He bowed his head as he passed, raised a handkerchief to his face, and called in a low voice, but clearly: "Hey, Doctor!"[9]

Both Lindbergh and Condon heard the voice.

As agreed, Condon gave the man, called Cemetery John, the ransom money with the recorded serial numbers. But Condon gave the man only one of the money packages, the one containing fifty thousand dollars.

Cemetery John then gave Condon a note that explained where to find the missing baby. Cemetery John disappeared and Condon returned to the car, giving Lindbergh the note and the remaining money. Although Condon had been instructed to wait six hours before reading the note, Lindbergh opened the note within minutes. It said that the baby was on a small boat off the Massachusetts coast and gave its location: "the boy is on the Boad [sic] Nelly . . . you will find the Boad [sic] between Horseneck Beach and Gay Head on Elizabeth Island."[10] Lindbergh and others spent days flying over the area, searching for a boat, but they found nothing. "We've been double-crossed," Lindbergh said.[11]

To further help the investigation, Condon wrote down and recorded on phonograph records all his conversations with Cemetery John. Condon also imitated the pronunciation and dialect, or the way Cemetery John spoke, which was with a strong German accent. A police artist drew sketches of Cemetery John from descriptions given by Condon and Joseph Perrone. Perrone was a taxi cab driver who had delivered a ransom letter from the kidnapper to Condon. A sketch of Cemetery John was given to FBI agents.

Cruel Hoaxes

Although Condon was honest in his dealings with Colonel and Mrs. Lindbergh, others were not. The Lindberghs and the police were busy dealing with several big kidnapping hoaxes.

Two hoaxes involved gangsters and bootleggers. Mickey Rosner, a bootlegger, claimed that because of his illegal connections, he could find the missing child quickly. Lindbergh accepted Rosner's offer and gave him money. Rosner was soon found to be a fraud. Another bootlegger and gangster, the notorious Al Capone, offered ten thousand dollars of his own money as a reward. He said he would help the Lindberghs find their child—but only if he was freed from prison. He was in jail for not paying federal taxes. The

Lindberghs finally refused Capone's offer because, said the IRS, "if released, Capone would immediately flee the country."[12]

By offering to help find little Charlie, Gaston Bullock Means, a former FBI agent turned conman, tried to cheat the Lindberghs and Evalyn Walsh McLean. McLean was the former wife of the publisher of the widely read newspaper the *Washington Post*. Means claimed that he knew the head of the kidnapping gang and that, if given one hundred thousand dollars, the gang would return the baby. To help the Lindberghs, McLean paid this money herself, plus extra. But Means had lied. For his theft, Means was jailed for fifteen years.

Another hoax involved John Hughes Curtis, a boatbuilder in Norfolk, Virginia. He claimed to have made contact with the leader of the gang that had stolen the baby. Like Means, he also lied, and finally confessed. He was fined and jailed for one year for giving false information and hindering a criminal investigation.

Charlie Is Found

On May 12, 1932, seventy-three days after Charlie Lindbergh was reported missing, he was found—dead—by a truck driver. His body was lying in a shallow grave and was covered by a pile of leaves. It was discovered four miles from the Lindberghs' house in the woods surrounding the home. He had died from a skull fracture and, according to the county physician who examined the body, had probably been dead since the night of the kidnapping. Nurse Betty Gow first identified the baby's body as that of little Charlie.

Colonel Lindbergh was checking another possible lead when he heard the sad news. He returned to New Jersey right away and identified his son. Then he went with the police to a crematorium in Linden, New Jersey. There the tiny body was cremated.

Now that the baby had been found, the investigation entered a new phase. The New Jersey State Police no longer had to be concerned about jeopardizing the child's safety. Now they could concentrate on finding who had kidnapped and murdered little Charlie. The police were kept busy for

Charlie Lindbergh was only two weeks old at the time of this photo.

many months, chasing down thousands of leads across the country.[13] The state of New Jersey offered a twenty-five-thousand-dollar reward for the capture of the baby's kidnappers.

Meanwhile, the Lindberghs' second child, Jon, was born on August 16, 1932. Crowds continued to mob the famous family when they appeared in public, offering condolences and suggestions on how to catch the kidnappers. Others, though, sent letters threatening to kidnap Jon.

Investigating Suspects

Over the next couple of months, the police intensely questioned the staffs of the Lindbergh and Morrow families as possible suspects. The police concentrated on Betty Gow and Violet Sharpe, the maid. Nurse Betty Gow was the last person to have seen Charlie Lindbergh alive. Earlier that evening, her boyfriend had telephoned her at the Lindberghs' home. The police questioned Gow and her boyfriend closely, finally concluding that the two had no part in the kidnapping.

Violet Sharpe was a maid in the Morrow household. When first asked by the police where she had been on the night of the kidnapping, Sharpe gave vague and inconsistent answers. On June 10, 1932, police telephoned Sharpe, to tell her they would be coming to ask her more questions. After the call, Sharpe committed suicide by taking cyanide, a strong poison.

Had Sharpe been involved in the kidnapping? The police finally said no, that Sharpe was in the clear. Later, more information about Sharpe surfaced. She had several boyfriends and went to a speakeasy regularly. In fact, on the night of little Charlie's abduction, she was at a speakeasy. She knew that the Morrows, her employers, would disapprove of such behavior and probably would have fired her, so it seemed that Sharpe had taken cyanide instead of talking with the police again.[14]

Appearance of the Ransom Money

The investigation into the kidnapping and murder of Charlie Lindbergh continued. On April 2, 1932, a few days after the ransom payment was made, a break came. That day, some of the ransom money appeared at a bank in upper Manhattan, New York City. The ransom money continued to appear, slowly but regularly, at various New York banks over the next several months. However, none of the bank employees could remember who had brought in the money. As more and more of the gold ransom bills showed up, the police kept a map on a wall, dotted with pins to represent where each bill had been spotted. By the fall of 1933, the police had established a pattern. Whoever was spending the ransom money seemed to be located in an area of the Bronx where many German-American people lived. Police officers began to regularly comb this area.

Their persistence paid off. On September 18, 1934, a teller at a Bronx bank noted a ten-dollar ransom bill with 4U-13-14 N.Y. penciled in the margin. (A gas station attendant had written the license plate number on the gold note thinking that it might be counterfeit.) This proved to be the license plate number for the owner of a dark 1930 Dodge car. The manager of the nearby gas station told the police that the customer, who spoke with a strong German accent, had bought gas for his car with the ten-dollar bill. The New York Motor Vehicle Bureau traced the license number to Bruno Richard Hauptmann, age thirty-five. A carpenter, German-born Hauptmann lived at 1279 East 222nd Street in the Bronx and owned a dark blue 1930 Dodge car. Hauptmann's address matched the area in which most of the ransom money had turned up. He also closely fit the description of Cemetery John as supplied by both Condon and Perrone.

On the morning of September 19, police followed Hauptmann as he drove off. After a few miles, one of the officers pulled Hauptmann over. Immediately a circle of police surrounded Hauptmann; all had their guns out. Without explaining why they had pulled Hauptmann over, the police handcuffed him, frisked him, and placed him under arrest. Checking his wallet, the police found some of the ransom money.

Hauptmann's Arrest

The police took Hauptmann to his modest second-story, five-room apartment. Hauptmann told the police that he had entered the United States illegally and worked as a carpenter. He was married to a German-born waitress named Anna. The couple had a son, almost a year old.

Hauptmann and his wife watched the police search their small apartment. When Anna Hauptmann asked her husband why the police were there, he lied. The police were there, he said, "about a gambling problem I had the other day."[15] One of the officers understood German and noted the lie. (No one knows for sure why Hauptmann lied. Perhaps he thought this explanation would be less upsetting to his wife than the truth, or perhaps he was guilty.)

The police saw that the apartment contained a lot of new, costly furniture. During their search, they found road maps of New Jersey and high-powered binoculars. When questioned by the police, Hauptmann denied having any more ransom money. However, the landlady turned over to the police Hauptmann's rent money for the month. He had paid the rent in cash and the money was more of the ransom bills. At quarter past noon, Hauptmann was arrested and taken to a New York police station in Manhattan. He did not have a lawyer and had not asked for one.

Who Was Hauptmann?

The police questioned Hauptmann intently, while other officers checked the writing on his automobile license application. Right away, they noted similarities between Hauptmann's writing and the writing in the ransom letters. When asked to provide writing samples, Hauptmann agreed. He wrote for hours for the police until he collapsed from exhaustion. Again, similarities were noted between Hauptmann's writing and the ransom notes, particularly in spelling and the way the letters were formed.

Officers continued to search Hauptmann's apartment. In one of Hauptmann's notebooks was a sketch of a ladder—

just like the one at the kidnapping site. The police inventoried Hauptmann's toolbox. It was complete except for the type of chisel left at the Lindbergh home. This type of chisel was a standard tool for a carpenter at this time.

The next morning, officers searched Hauptmann's small garage. Inside the garage, behind a board nailed above the workbench, a detective found two packets wrapped in newspaper. Both packets contained ransom money. The police

Based on witnesses' descriptions, the police made these sketches of the baby's kidnapper.

then uncovered a hidden shelf containing more ransom money. Hauptmann continued to tell the police that he had no more ransom money, until he was confronted with what the police had found.

At this point, Hauptmann changed his story. Now he told the police that he had been holding the money for Isidor Fisch, a German-born friend and business partner. In December 1933, just before leaving the United States for Germany, Fisch had given him a shoebox full of money. Since Fisch, said Hauptmann, owed him money, Hauptmann began to take money from the shoebox. Fisch died soon after he returned to Germany.

The police continued to question Hauptmann. During this questioning, they sometimes withheld food and water for long periods. Hauptmann was not allowed to sleep for three days, except when he dozed off between questioning sessions. The police also beat Hauptmann. Hauptmann never confessed to the kidnapping or murder of Charlie Lindbergh during the questioning.

Hauptmann told the police he could not remember what he was doing the night of the kidnapping. He also said he did not have a criminal record. This, however, was a lie. Born on November 26, 1899, in Saxony, Germany, Hauptmann had committed a series of armed robberies, had been in prison, and had escaped from prison several times. He had stowed away on ships coming to America two times, but each time he had been returned to Germany. In November 1923, to avoid going to jail for his latest burglaries, Hauptmann stowed away aboard a ship coming to

America once again. This time, he ended up in New York City illegally. He married Anna Schoeffler, a German-born New York waitress, on October 10, 1925. On November 23, 1933, the couple had a son.

While in America, Hauptmann worked as a carpenter. Soon after March 1, 1932, the date of the kidnapping, his finances improved a great deal and he worked only part time or not at all. Although he appeared to no longer have a regular income, he was still able to buy furniture and clothing, go on hunting trips, buy stocks in the stock market, and pay for a trip to Germany for his wife.

While the questioning of Hauptmann went on, teams of police continued to search his apartment and garage. They found Condon's address and telephone number written in pencil on the trim of a closet door. They also discovered more ransom money and a small loaded pistol.

Since John F. Condon had seen and spoken to the alleged kidnapper when he handed over the ransom money, the police asked him to identify Hauptmann in a lineup. This line of people, including the suspect, was arranged by the police for identification by witnesses. Condon looked at the men, then picked Hauptmann out of the lineup. Condon then asked Hauptmann some questions. But afterward, when the police pressed Condon for a positive identification of Hauptmann, Condon said that he could not do this.

Steps in a Criminal Case

The case against Hauptmann, a suspected criminal, followed specific legal procedures. Although the sequence of steps varies from state to state, here is the usual procedure followed in a suspected criminal case:

Arrest. After police investigate a crime, they file a report describing the crime and name a suspect or suspects. Police arrest the suspects. Upon arrest, suspects are informed of their rights.

Booking. At the police station, suspects are searched, photographed, fingerprinted, and allowed to contact a lawyer. Suspects are usually jailed.

Initial Court Appearance. At the initial court appearance, the judge informs the suspects of the charge against them and their rights. A judge is a public official who hears and decides cases in a court of law. The judge also decides if the suspects should be released on bail or kept in jail. Bail is the release of an arrested person in exchange for money and a promise to appear in court later. The suspects' next court date is set.

Preliminary Hearing. A preliminary hearing is called for suspects accused of felonies. A felony is a serious crime, such as murder. A convicted felon is generally punished by imprisonment or by death. If the judge decides there is enough evidence at the preliminary hearing, the case is forwarded to a grand jury.

Grand Jury Indictment. The grand jury decides if enough evidence exists for the accused to stand trial. If it votes yes, a court order called an indictment is issued requiring the suspects to stand trial.

Arraignment. The judge reads the charges to the

accused, who are again advised of their rights. The accused then plead guilty or not guilty. If:

- Not guilty, a date is set for the trial.

- They plead guilty, a trial is not held. Instead a date is set for sentencing.

Pretrial Hearing. The judge meets with the attorneys from both sides and reviews the issues of the case.

Trial. The accused, now called the defendants, stand trial before a jury, a group of people who have sworn to decide the facts in a court case and to reach a fair decision. A trial is a formal presentation of both sides of a case before a jury.

In a criminal case, the state has the burden of proof. This means the state must persuade the jury that enough facts exist to prove that the defendant is guilty of the crime.

Verdict. After hearing the evidence and testimony in the case, the jury reaches a verdict, or final decision. If:

- Not guilty, the defendants are free.

- Guilty, the defendants receive a sentencing, or punishment.

Sentence. At the end of a criminal trial, the jury or judge decides the punishment.

Rights of Criminals

When someone is arrested and tried on a criminal charge, that person's rights are protected by several amendments to the United States Constitution. These amendments include many safeguards to ensure that the criminal procedures are fair. In the Constitution, these safeguards are part of the amendments that make up the Bill of Rights. The Bill of Rights contains the first ten amendments to the United States Constitution. It protects the rights of individuals.

Fourth Amendment. Protects against:

1. Unwarranted search and seizure of property or person. The person must give permission or the state must have a search warrant.

2. Being arrested without probable cause. Probable cause occurs when the state can demonstrate that the police knew enough at the time of the arrest to believe that an offense had been committed and that the defendant likely committed it. The defendant is the person accused of committing the crime.

Fifth Amendment. Gives the accused the right to remain silent during questioning, protecting against self-incrimination. This means the accused can refuse to answer questions subjecting them to accusation of a crime.

Sixth Amendment. Gives the accused the right to:

1. A lawyer to represent them in court.

2. A speedy public trial with a fair or impartial (not biased) jury.

3. Be informed of all charges.

4. Present witnesses in their favor.

5. Cross-examine the government's witnesses. Cross-examination is the questioning of the opposition's witnesses.

Eighth Amendment. Protects against cruel and unusual punishment if convicted and sentenced for a crime.

Hauptmann's Pretrial Steps

Since Hauptmann had been arrested in New York City, his case was first heard by the grand jury of the Supreme Court, Bronx County, New York. The case started on September 24, 1934. The grand jury listened to several dozen witnesses testify. Hauptmann also testified. He said he was not Cemetery John and had not received ransom money in a cemetery. Instead, he had been at home with his wife and a friend. He admitted that he had written Condon's address and telephone number on the trim of his closet door. Why? He told the grand jury that he had done this because he had been following the case.

Charles Lindbergh, in disguise, came to the grand jury hearing. Previously, he had told the police that he would not be able to recognize the voice he heard at the cemetery. But as he listened to Hauptmann, Lindbergh reversed himself. During the grand jury hearing, Lindbergh testified that Hauptmann had called out, "Hey Doctor! Hey Doctor! Over here!" on April 2, 1932, the night the ransom money had been exchanged.[16]

On October 8, 1934, the twenty-three members of the grand jury deliberated, or discussed the case, for less than thirty minutes. Although no one had seen the kidnapping or murder of the baby, the grand jury voted to indict Hauptmann for the murder of the Lindbergh baby. An indictment is a formal, written accusation that outlines what crimes are believed to have been committed. It also names the person who probably committed the crime.

One more step was needed to get Hauptmann tried for murder in New Jersey, where the crime had been committed. On October 15 Hauptmann's extradition hearing was held before Judge Ernest E. L. Hammer. An extradition is the surrender of an alleged criminal by one state to another having the jurisdiction, or legal authority, to try the case. Under New Jersey law at that time, kidnapping carried a jail sentence of five to thirty years. Murder could bring a sentence of death. Judge Hammer soon announced that Hauptmann would be extradited to New Jersey to stand trial for murder.

On October 19, Hauptmann was moved from his prison cell to a police car. Three police cars drove in front and three more followed behind. Hauptmann's car was also escorted by police on motorcycles. The destination was Flemington in Hunterdon County, New Jersey—a small, quiet town of some twenty-seven hundred people—away from the crowds in Hopewell. Upon his arrival, the media and curious onlookers mobbed Hauptmann. Flashbulbs popped and questions flew.

Hauptmann was put into the Flemington jail. A guard shared his cell and two others were close by. As part of a twenty-four-hour suicide watch, Hauptmann's cell was lit constantly.

The Judge and Jury

On October 23, 1934, Judge Thomas W. Trenchard arraigned Hauptmann on the charge of murder. During an arraignment, the judge reads the charges to the accused and advises the accused of his or her rights. The judge then set the trial to start on January 2, 1935.

During a trial, the judge should be impartial. He or she should not take sides. The duties of a judge include the following:

- listening to evidence,

- making certain the accused's constitutional rights are protected,

- making sure that proper legal procedures are followed, and

- listening when the lawyers argue over evidence, then deciding, on the basis of rules of evidence, whether the evidence should be admitted into the trial.

Before a trial officially begins, a jury of twelve people is selected by the judge and lawyers for both sides. This process began on January 2, 1935. Jury selection for Hauptmann's trial went smoothly. Four women and eight men were selected.

All jurors must be impartial. They must not be biased against the defendant. The duties of a jury include the following:

- evaluating the evidence presented at the trial,

- deciding if the accused is guilty beyond a reasonable doubt. Reasonable doubt is the highest level of certainty a juror must have in the court system to find a defendant guilty of a crime.

- reaching a unanimous decision after hearing all the evidence at the trial, and

- announcing the verdict, or decision, to the accused and judge.

Because of the immense media interest in the case, the jury members were not allowed to go home. Instead, they stayed at Flemington's only hotel. During the trial, jury members were not allowed to read newspaper articles about the case. They also could not see or talk about the trial with anyone. But the jury could still hear other people discuss the trial when they ate in the hotel's main dining room each day, separated from other diners by only a cloth curtain.

Media Frenzy

During winter 1935, Hauptmann's trial continually made front-page headline news alongside other important events: the Great Depression, Adolf Hitler's rise in Germany, gangsters and their crimes, and President Roosevelt's efforts to end the Depression. The day before the trial, sixty thousand people flooded into Flemington. Included in the mob were seven hundred reporters; hundreds of radio broadcasters, cameramen, writers, photographers, and telegraph operators; and thousands of sightseers. Over a hundred telegraph lines were set up in Flemington.

The trial quickly turned into a form of entertainment. It became a society event, a place to be seen and to be admired for the attendance of famous singers, sports figures, movie stars, comedians, and novelists. The courtroom was usually packed with hundreds of people. Hundreds more who could

Public Notices 165

ANYONE knowing whereabouts of George McMahon, who disappeared March 19, 1925, kindly notify his wife, Helen McMahon, of 257 Hudson st. Has brown eyes, brown hair, dark complexion; age 52.

I WILL not be responsible for any debts contracted except by myself after this

LETTER received at new address. Will follow your instructions. I also received letter mailed to me March 4, and was ready since then. Please hurry on account of mother. Address me to the address you mention in your letter. Father.

Transportation

SPECIAL MARCH Packards, Cadillacs, Lincolns Leave Daily

MIAMI Chicago California Times Sq.

anna 4-74

WO. work. 7-8569.

WOMAN, Ger part time, 1676 1st ave

WOMAN, you home; refer Henry st., Br

WOMAN (yo nything. Wo x 366.

YUNG WOM usekeeper, hly recon 5. 1969 Je

UNG Swed days week. ave.

YOUNG GIRL wants work

Househol

ABLE day Ag

Notices

ANEY call 236 E. 30th st. ress. Mother.

I WILL no be responsible for any debts contr T. ood.

MONEY IS READY—JAFSIE.

MY WIFE, Mary Newkirk (Mary Warren) left my bed and board not Carl Newkirk.

35
75
75
35
68

70
20
55
60
25
4

8.

W.

Colonel Lindbergh and John Condon used a combination of newspaper ads and letters to arrange for Charlie's return in exchange for ransom money. In these ads, Lindbergh identified himself as "Father" and Condon was known as "Jafsie."

not get a seat stood in the aisles, along the walls, or hung over the courtroom balcony. Others who were not as lucky watched from outside, pressing their faces up against the windows.

Con artists were there, too. In the streets by the courthouse, people sold clumps of blond hair, supposedly from the Lindbergh baby. Photos of the Lindberghs also sold well. So did scale models of the kidnapper's ladder, priced at ten cents.

Hauptmann could hear the street commotion in his cell. The guard on duty for New Year's Day reported that Hauptmann "spent most of his waking hours for the last day and a half pacing up and down. . . . He also had a worried expression."[17]

From the first day, the press sensationalized the trial. Direct broadcasting of the trial was not allowed because microphones and cameras were banned in the courtroom during the trial. But there was plenty of minute-by-minute trial coverage, thanks to reporters taking notes during the proceedings.

The world's largest telephone system was assembled during the trial, with over a million words a day leaving Flemington.[18] Newspapers across the country ran many articles and photos. Often, several pages were filled with information about the trial. Television had just been invented, but there was no lack of daily trial coverage by television stations as well as newspapers and radio stations. Photographers stood on tables in the courtroom, vying for good shots. During the trial, reporters sitting behind Hauptmann would poke and taunt him.

One magazine later summed up the circuslike atmosphere. "For two months the world went mad and the center of the universe shifted to the sleepy town of Flemington. All sense of proportion and much of the sense of decency was lost."[19]

This was the emotionally charged setting when Bruno Richard Hauptmann's trial began on January 3, 1935.

chapter four

THE CASE FOR NEW JERSEY

FLEMINGTON—Bruno Richard Hauptmann's trial began on a cold, snowy Wednesday morning, on January 3, 1935. In a criminal case involving murder, the state accuses and prosecutes, or brings to trial, the suspected criminal. The state of New Jersey charged Bruno Richard Hauptmann with the murder of Charles Augustus Lindbergh, Jr. The case, called the *State of New Jersey* v. *Bruno Richard Hauptmann*, was argued in one million, six hundred words, and would fill thirty typewritten volumes or books.

The Trial Process

To present the facts and support arguments during a trial, lawyers for each side call witnesses. These people come to the witness stand and take an oath, promising to give truthful testimony or information. Sometimes one or both sides hire expert witnesses. These people have specialized knowledge of a subject and are allowed to testify about that knowledge in court. Each side can also present evidence. Evidence is any physical item relevant to the trial. This can include documents, maps, guns, letters, and other objects related to the case.

During a criminal trial, both sides—the prosecution or state first, followed by the defense—present their witnesses and evidence to the jury. The prosecutor is a government official authorized to accuse and prosecute (bring to trial) someone who is believed to have committed a crime. During this process, witnesses are asked questions. Each side calls its own witnesses and questions them on direct examination. This means that they may ask only "direct questions" or open-ended questions that do not suggest a specific answer. For example, "Where were you at 10:00 P.M. on April 15, 1931?" is a direct question.

The prosecuting lawyers present their witnesses and evidence first. The prosecutors try to convince the jury that the defendant is guilty of the charge. The defense then questions the prosecution's witnesses to try to show that the witnesses are not believable, are incorrect, or are prejudiced against the defendant. This is called cross-examination.

The Prosecution's Strategy

No one had seen the kidnapping or the murder and, so far, Hauptmann had not confessed to the crime. So the prosecution built its case for first-degree murder against Hauptmann mostly on circumstantial evidence, evidence that tries to prove a fact by showing that other events or circumstances *seem* to connect the defendant to the crime. First degree murder is murder that was thought out before it was committed. The prosecution's strongest evidence included:

- Handwriting evidence, including the ransom notes;

- The ransom money found in Hauptmann's garage;

- The handmade ladder left at the crime scene (and Hauptmann's ability as a carpenter to have made it);

- Witnesses who testified that they had seen Hauptmann in the following places:

  - Near the Lindbergh home just prior to March 1, 1932, the night of the kidnapping; and

  - At the cemetery, where he taken the ransom money.

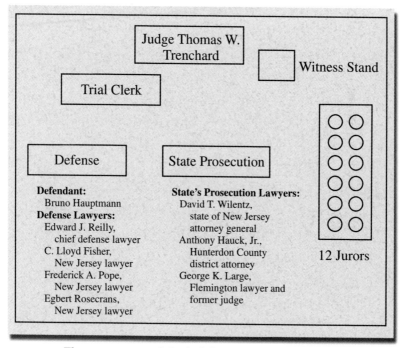

The courtroom as it looked during Hauptmann's trial.

The Prosecution's Opening Statement

On January 3, the court crier announced Judge Trenchard, and everyone in the courtroom stood as the judge entered the courtroom. Seventy-one-year-old Judge Trenchard had a solid record—none of his decisions in a murder trial had ever been reversed. Judge Trenchard told the jury not to read the newspapers, listen to the radio, or attend any public assembly. He then ordered the trial to begin.

Hauptmann's trial officially began with an opening statement by the prosecution. Opening statements summarize the strong points of each side's case and what each side intends to prove during the trial. However, nothing the lawyers say during the opening is considered evidence.

The packed courtroom heard the prosecutor, Attorney General David T. Wilentz, say that in New Jersey, if anyone commits a burglary and kills someone during the burglary, then that is considered murder in the first degree. Wilentz said that the state would prove that Hauptmann had kidnapped and murdered the Lindbergh baby, written the ransom notes, and taken ransom money from Dr. John Condon. Wilentz then launched into his version of how Hauptmann had committed the kidnapping and murder. "He came there with his ladder, placed it against that house. He broke into and entered at night the Lindbergh home with the intent to steal that child and its clothing. And he did."[1]

Next he described the discovery of the missing child, Hauptmann's arrest, and the evidence found in Hauptmann's apartment and garage. He supplied a motive, or reason, for the crime. Hauptmann, he said, had committed this crime for "money, money, money."[2] Finishing, he told the jury that the state would prove all the facts in the case, then asked the jury to give Hauptmann the death penalty for his crime. After Wilentz finished, some spectators applauded.

Defense lawyer Edward Reilly stood and asked the judge to declare "a mistrial on the impassioned appeal of the attorney general, not being a proper opening, but merely a summation and a desire to inflame the minds of this jury. . . ."[3] A mistrial is a trial that has no legal effect because of some error or serious misconduct by one of the parties involved. Judge Trenchard refused to declare a mistrial, but told the jury to listen to all the evidence presented and to be fair during the trial.

The New York police took these photographs of Bruno Richard Hauptmann shortly after his arrest.

Prosecution's Witnesses

The prosecution had eighty-seven witnesses testify during the trial. Some testified about the events during the time of the kidnapping and the ransom payment, while others testified about seeing Hauptmann near the scene of the crime or being associated with the ransom money. The prosecution also called various experts to the witness stand to testify about key evidence—the ladder, the ransom money, and handwriting evidence.

The Lindberghs. One of the first witnesses on the stand was Mrs. Anne Lindbergh. Attorney General Wilentz had her describe the evening of March 1, 1932, the date of the kidnapping. After that, she identified clothing found on the dead child. These were tagged as evidence in the case. Reilly, the defense attorney, had no questions for her. He said, "The defense feels that the grief of Mrs. Lindbergh needs no cross-examination."[4]

Colonel Lindbergh testified next. He described what happened the night of the kidnapping, then talked about the unusual noise he had heard that evening. Wilentz read the first ransom note to the jury, which was submitted as evidence. Lindbergh discussed his partnership with John Condon, including the exchange of ransom money.

Wilentz then asked Lindbergh if he had been near St. Raymond's Cemetery on the night of April 2, 1932. Lindbergh said yes, he had been there. Wilentz then asked if Lindbergh could identify the person who had called out to Condon that night. Before he answered, Lindbergh turned

John. He again described what he had told the police, that the man had "muddy blond hair and deep-set eyes, high cheekbones, a small mouth and pointed chin, a pale complexion, and a heavy accent" and was "wiry and muscular."[12] Condon had given this same description more than two years before at Hauptmann's arrest. Condon's description fit Hauptmann well.

During cross-examination, the defense could not discredit Condon's testimony. When Condon left the courthouse after testifying, a waiting crowd cheered him.

Other Eyewitnesses. The prosecution had a surprise witness—Hildegarde Alexander, a blonde fashion model. She was acquainted with Dr. Condon. Wearing a fur coat and hat at the trial, the young woman testified that in March 1932, she had seen Hauptmann following Dr. Condon in a Bronx railroad station. She testified that this man, whom she later identified as Hauptmann, had closely watched Condon. This incident had occurred before the ransom money had been paid.

Hauptmann had claimed to be at work as a carpenter on the day of the kidnapping and on the day of the ransom payment. A Manhattan building superintendent testified that Hauptmann was not at work on either of these days. Other witnesses identified Hauptmann, including two men who said they saw Hauptmann near Hopewell on the day of the kidnapping.

Relatives of Isidor Fisch, Hauptmann's friend who supposedly owed him money, came from Germany to testify for the prosecution. They said that Isidor Fisch had died nearly penniless four months after he returned to Germany. Fisch did not have much money and actually owed several people money, including Hauptmann. In fact, Fisch had borrowed money from Hauptmann for his trip to Germany. This testimony was in direct contrast to what Hauptmann had said at his grand jury hearing.

Cecile Barr, a cashier at a Manhattan movie theater, testified that on November 26, 1933, Hauptmann had paid for his ticket with a five-dollar ransom bill folded "three times in eight parts."[13] The next morning, the well-creased bill was deposited at a nearby bank. A teller noticed it was one of the

Colonel Lindbergh took this photo of Charlie on his first birthday.

ransom bills and informed the police. When Barr came to work that evening, the police questioned her about the man who had given her the bill.

Barr described Hauptmann, a man of medium height and medium build in his mid-thirties. He had blue eyes, high cheek bones, flat cheeks, and a pointed chin. The police showed Barr a drawing of Hauptmann, which was based on information from Condon and Perrone. Yes, she said, that was the man who had given her the money for the movie.

Barr's testimony was critical to the prosecution's case. The date of November 26, 1933, was a full month before Isidor Fisch had sailed to Germany. Through Barr's testimony, the prosecution showed that Hauptmann had lied about when he actually had possession of the ransom money. Her testimony also raised serious doubt about Hauptmann's claim of receiving ransom money from Fisch.

Key Evidence

The prosecution called many experts to the witness stand to testify on the powerful circumstantial evidence against Hauptmann. The prosecution used three main areas of evidence in its case: handwriting evidence, the ransom money, and the ladder.

Handwriting Evidence. Seven handwriting experts testified that Hauptmann had written all fifteen of the ransom notes, including the first one found in the nursery. The first handwriting expert called to the witness stand was Albert S. Osborn, the nation's authority in the field and author of various books on the subject. During his testimony, he often referred to a large rack that held clear, large photographs of key words and letters. The photographs were also passed among the jury. The photographed words and letters were in the ransom notes and Hauptmann's known writing. Hauptmann's known writing included automobile registration applications, an insurance application, notebooks, and the words he had been asked to write in the police station.

Osborn pointed out many similarities between the ransom notes and Hauptmann's handwriting. These included unusual spelling of common words and transposed letters in words. According to Osborn, there were dozens of matches found between Hauptmann's handwriting samples and the handwriting in the ransom notes.

Hauptmann, continued Osborn, seldom crossed his *t's* or dotted his *i's* in his own handwriting. These same patterns continually appeared in the ransom notes. And, in both cases, some letters were formed in unusual ways, such as inverted uppercase *N's* and *Y's* that looked like *J's*. Further,

Word Correctly Spelled	How the Word Appeared in Hauptmann's Samples and Ransom Notes
house	haus
not	note
anything	anyding
good	gut
boat	boad
light	lihgt
right	rihgt

said Osborn, one man had written all the ransom notes. Osborn concluded by saying, the fact that Hauptmann had written the ransom notes was "irresistible, unanswerable and overwhelming."[14]

John F. Tyrrell was another handwriting expert. With a crayon, he drew some of the similar letters in Hauptmann's handwriting and the ransom notes, such as the letters *x*, *t*, and *y*, and the hyphenated *New-York*. When the defense, on cross-examination, said that there was no similarity in some letters, Tyrrell would not back down.

Harry M. Cassidy, a documents examiner, was also certain that Hauptmann had written the ransom notes. He testified, "I am obligated to say the person who wrote those request writings [for the police] is the same person who wrote all those ransom notes."[15]

Clark Sellers, another documents examiner, testified that Hauptmann's handwriting was so distinctive, he "might as well have signed the notes with his own name."[16] The other three handwriting experts agreed that all ransom notes had been written by the same person. The handwriting experts for the state "resulted in a virtually unanimous opinion that all the notes were written by the same person" and that the German-born writer had lived in the United States for some time.[17]

Ransom Money

The ransom currency bills were called gold notes. Unlike regular green currency bills, a gold note had a round yellow seal. This made it easy to spot any ransom money if someone was spending it.

Frank Wilson, an Internal Revenue Service agent, testified that he had been in charge of preparing the ransom money. After the ransom had been paid, the government had distributed over two hundred fifty thousand lists of the serial numbers to banks across the country. Wilson identified $14,600 in gold notes as Lindbergh ransom money—these were the bills found in Hauptmann's garage. Finally, Wilson testified that since Hauptmann's arrest, no more ransom money had appeared. Wilson's testimony was strong evidence for the prosecution.

The Ladder

The prosecution used the ladder found at the Lindberghs' home as an essential piece of evidence connecting Hauptmann to the crime. Arthur Koehler, age forty-seven, was the prosecution's star expert witness. Koehler was the chief wood-identification expert for the United States government. He had written a book called *The Properties and Uses of Wood*, as well as many articles and booklets on the subject. Long before Hauptmann's arrest, Koehler had studied the ladder for many months. He had gone to lumber mills across the country, trying to match wood pieces used in making the ladder.

Before Koehler begin testifying, defense lawyer Frederick Pope stood and told the judge that no one could be called a wood expert since this was a science never recognized in a courtroom before. Judge Trenchard said that

Koehler was qualified as a wood technologist, which made him an expert witness. Pope sat down and the trial continued.

Koehler testified one of the boards used to make the ladder matched a plank, or piece of wood, that was missing from Hauptmann's attic floor. The board in question, he said, was rail sixteen on the ladder. Koehler used photo enlargements and drawings of the boards and wood to show strong similarities between rail sixteen and the missing plank. He testified, "Those two pieces [of wood] at one time were one piece. They have been cut in two."[18]

Bruno Richard Hauptmann (center front) in the Hunterdon County Courthouse is flanked by a guard (left front) and Edward Reilly, his chief defense lawyer (right front).

According to Koehler, Hauptmann had run out of wood when he was building the ladder. So, he sawed a piece from his attic floor. When Koehler tested Hauptmann's tools, including a plane, on similar wood, the tools left distinct marks on the wood. These marks, said Koehler, matched those on the ladder. Koehler also testified about how he had traced the origins of the wood for rail sixteen to a Bronx lumber store a year before Hauptmann's arrest. Then he explained and showed how one of Hauptmann's wood chisels could have been used to make the ladder. Hauptmann's chisel was the same type of chisel found underneath the nursery window.

Koehler testified that since Hauptmann was a skilled carpenter, he could have designed and built the ladder. In fact, Koehler said, only a carpenter had the skills necessary to build the ladder. The crudely built but lightweight ladder was in three sections and could be taken apart and put together quickly.

Wilentz then asked Koehler if he had taken the ladder apart and put it into Hauptmann's car. Yes, Koehler had done this several times. The pieces all fit and there was even extra room inside the car.

The defense lawyer, on cross-examination, challenged most of what Koehler had said. But Koehler stuck to the results of his exhaustive research—that North Carolina pine from a lumber store near Hauptmann's home and a board cut from Hauptmann's attic were used to make the kidnapping ladder. After Koehler testified, *The New York Times* wrote, "You shuddered at the thought of what might happen to you if such a mind . . . should get to work upon your own remote past—a man who searched 1,900 factories for traces of the scratches of your plane on a piece of wood. It was fantastic and horrifying."[19]

Prosecution Ends Its Case

After Koehler stepped from the witness stand, Wilentz stood and said that the prosecution had ended its case. It had taken the state seventeen days to present all of its witnesses and evidence.

After Wilentz sat down, the defense asked the judge to acquit, or completely discharge, the case. Judge Trenchard denied the request. Now it was the defense's turn to call its witnesses to the stand.

chapter five

THE CASE FOR BRUNO HAUPTMANN

COURTROOM—The state had presented a great deal of strong circumstantial evidence against Bruno Richard Hauptmann. The defense had a big job ahead, to try and counter this mountain of evidence. The defense used Hauptmann as its principal witness. For seventeen hours, while he was on the witness stand, Hauptmann answered question after question. He denied any and all involvement with the crime. Following his testimony, the defense called a series of questionable witnesses.

The Defense's Strategy

The defense lawyers were:

- Edward J. Reilly, chief defense lawyer, from Brooklyn, New York;

- C. Lloyd Fisher, New Jersey lawyer;

- Frederick A. Pope, New Jersey lawyer; and

- Egbert Rosecrans, New Jersey lawyer.

The defense tried to prove that Hauptmann was not guilty of murder. Its proof came in three main areas:

- Witnesses for the

defense would testify that Hauptmann was elsewhere during the kidnapping and ransom money exchange.

- Expert witnesses would show that Hauptmann had not written the ransom notes.

- The ladder had been mishandled since Hauptmann's arrest and should not be used as evidence in the case.

The Defense's Opening Statement

The courtroom was packed with members of the media and spectators when Lloyd Fisher gave the opening statement for the defense. For thirty minutes, he described what the defense would prove. Hauptmann, Fisher said, had alibis for three key dates—the night of the kidnapping, the date of the ransom exchange, and the night the theater cashier testified that he had given her ransom money for a ticket. An alibi is a legal defense by which a defendant tries to prove he or she was not present at the scene of a crime.

Fisher continued his key points. He said that the defense had its own handwriting experts. These experts would cast doubt on what the prosecution's handwriting experts had to say about Hauptmann's writing. However, Fisher said, the defense could not produce as many regular and expert witnesses as the prosecution. Why? The defense could not afford to pay for so many witnesses.

Finally, Fisher told the jury that the ladder had been mishandled so much since Hauptmann's arrest that it was now worthless evidence. In fact, said Fisher, the New Jersey State Police had mishandled the entire case: "No case in all of history was as badly handled or as managed."[1] The defense attorney also vowed to prove that many of the prosecution's witnesses were not credible or trustworthy.

Defense's Witnesses

To the press, the defense had promised that many witnesses would testify. Yet, only a fraction of these defense witnesses actually showed up. A few, particularly the expert witnesses, helped Hauptmann's case. However, most of the defense witnesses were not credible.

Bruno Richard Hauptmann—Direct Examination. After Fisher finished, Reilly stood and asked Bruno Richard Hauptmann to be sworn in and to take the witness stand. As Hauptmann walked to the witness stand, one of his guards followed, then stood behind the witness chair. Other guards stood by the jury box, the judge's box, beneath the courtroom windows, and beside his wife, Anna Hauptmann. This was the first time that Hauptmann had testified at his trial and he was the defense's key witness. He would testify for a total of seventeen hours.

In broken English, Hauptmann answered Reilly's questions about his life in Germany. Hauptmann went on to talk about how he had met Anna, and worked hard while in the United States. Both husband and wife worked regularly, he as a carpenter and she as a bakery clerk and helper. Both were able to save money. They put some of their savings in the bank and some they put in a safe place at home.

Reilly moved on to a critical time—the days shortly before the kidnapping and the day of the kidnapping. Hauptmann testified that he had gotten carpentry work at the

WANTED

INFORMATION AS TO THE WHEREABOUTS OF

CHAS. A. LINDBERGH, Jr.

OF HOPEWELL, N. J.

SON OF COL. CHAS. A. LINDBERGH

World-Famous Aviator

This child was kidnaped from his home in Hopewell, N. J., between 8 and 10 p. m. on Tuesday, March 1, 1932.

DESCRIPTION:

Age, 20 months   Hair, blond, curly
Weight, 27 to 30 lbs.   Eyes, dark blue
Height, 29 inches   Complexion, light
Deep dimple in center of chin
Dressed in one-piece coverall night suit

ADDRESS ALL COMMUNICATIONS TO
COL. H. N. SCHWARZKOPF, TRENTON, N. J., or
COL. CHAS. A. LINDBERGH, HOPEWELL, N. J.

ALL COMMUNICATIONS WILL BE TREATED IN CONFIDENCE

March 11, 1932

COL. H. NORMAN SCHWARZKOPF
Supt. New Jersey State Police, Trenton, N. J.

The New Jersey State Police distributed this wanted poster to find the kidnapped baby.

Majestic, an apartment house, on Saturday, February 27, 1932. The job, Hauptmann said, started on Tuesday, March 1, 1932. When he reported to work on that day, he was told that he could not start until March 15. He returned then, and worked until Saturday, April 2. He quit on April 2 because the company was not paying him the promised salary. Reilly asked Hauptmann a series of questions to establish that Hauptmann had, in fact, been at the Majestic all day on April 2. The exchange of the ransom money had occurred on April 2, 1932, in the evening.

Reilly then asked Hauptmann to account for all of his time on April 2. Hauptmann testified that he had worked from 7:00 A.M. until 5:00 P.M. that day, then left for home. By six o'clock, he was home and an hour later, the Hauptmanns were entertaining a friend, Hans Kloeppenburg, who had come to their apartment. Kloeppenburg stayed until nearly midnight. Reilly summed up this important testimony by having Hauptmann explain that he never had left his apartment after he came home at 6:00 P.M. on April 2.

At this point, Reilly asked Hauptmann if he had kidnapped Charles Lindbergh, Jr. Hauptmann denied that he had committed this crime. He also denied being in Hopewell, New Jersey, or near the Lindbergh's home on March 1, 1932.

Under Reilly's questioning, Hauptmann described how he had met and become friends with Isidor Fisch. The night before Fisch left for Germany, he had given Hauptmann a small box. Hauptmann did not look inside the box until

August 1934. Inside he found a great deal of money which he began to spend because Fisch owed him money.

At Reilly's request, a court attendant placed the three sections of the ladder in front of Hauptmann and the jury. Reilly asked Hauptmann if he had built the ladder. Hauptmann responded by saying, "I am a carpenter."[2] The crowd started laughing. Raising his voice over the noise, Reilly repeated his question. This time, Hauptmann denied that he had built the ladder and jeered that the ladder looked like a " 'moosic' [music] instrument."[3]

When questioned further by Reilly, Hauptmann denied that he had been in St. Raymond's Cemetery on April 2, 1932. Nor, he testified, had he received fifty thousand dollars or any money from Dr. Condon. Reilly brought up the remaining critical date, November 26, 1933. This was the night, according to Cecile Barr, a movie theater cashier, that Hauptmann had paid for his ticket with a well-folded five-dollar ransom bill. That night, Hauptmann said, he had stayed at home. Since November 26 was his birthday, he and his wife, along with several friends, had celebrated all evening at the Hauptmanns' apartment.

Reilly moved on with his questioning. What about Hildegarde Alexander's testimony that in March 1932 she had seen Hauptmann following Dr. Condon in a Bronx railroad station? Impossible, said Hauptmann. He had never been inside that station. Next, Reilly had Hauptmann talk a little about his stock market investments and finances.

Now came the time when Hauptmann made the first mistake in his testimony. After Hauptmann testified about his arrest and treatment at the police station, Reilly asked about the handwriting samples at the police station. Hauptmann testified that during the first night at the police station, police told him what to write down. Reilly next asked if Hauptmann had spelled everything himself or whether the police told him how to spell certain words. Hauptmann testified that, "Some of them words they spell it to me."[4]

To drive home this point, Reilly asked Hauptmann, "How do you spell *signature?*" Hauptmann spelled, "*S-I-G-N-U-T-U-R-E.*"

Continuing along, Reilly asked, "Did they tell you to spell it '*S-I-N-G*—?'"[5] Yes, said Hauptmann, the police had told him how to write this word incorrectly.

Reilly used the word *signature* in his question-and-answer exchange with Hauptmann because it had appeared in the ransom notes. However, although Hauptmann had testified that the police had told him to misspell this word, the police had never asked him to write this word. Further, Hauptmann had misspelled *signature* while on the witness stand. He had spelled it the same way it had appeared in the ransom letters.

Soon Hauptmann made another serious mistake. By this point in the trial, he had testified that the police had beaten him: "I got a couple of knocks in the ribs when I refused to write."[6] His beating was not questioned because it was a known truth. But Hauptmann had said that he had willingly given writing samples because the samples would clear him of the crime. Based on this confusing testimony, the jury was left wondering if Hauptmann had willingly supplied the writing samples for the police or had refused until beaten.[7]

Bruno Richard Hauptmann—Cross Examination. Prosecutor David Wilentz began his cross-examination by having Hauptmann talk about his criminal record in Germany. Hauptmann testified that he was a convicted felon (someone who committed a serious crime) and had spent nearly four years in a German prison. Wilentz then had Hauptmann explain his illegal entry into the United States and that he lived in America illegally.

After this, Wilentz walked to the prosecution table and picked up a notebook that belonged to Hauptmann. It was a journal of sorts and it contained notes that covered the year 1931. Opening the notebook, Wilentz asked Hauptmann to spell the word *boat*, which Hauptmann correctly did. At this point in the trial, Wilentz held the notebook out to Hauptmann and pointed to a particular word. "Why did you spell it *B-O-A-D*?"[8] Hauptmann could not give a satisfactory answer. The word *boat*, spelled as *boad*, had been used in the ransom letters.

Wilentz continued to point out to the jury and Hauptmann other misspellings in Hauptmann's notebooks. He compared these words to the same misspellings in the ransom letters. Wilentz showed other similarities between Hauptmann's handwriting and the ransom notes. *New York* was hyphenated, for example. The *g* and *h* were reversed in words such as *right* and *light*. Hauptmann offered no explanation for the similarities.

In another of Hauptmann's notebooks, Wilentz paged to

a drawing of a ladder. This drawing closely resembled the kidnapper's ladder. Wilentz showed Hauptmann this drawing, asking if he had drawn it. Hauptmann denied that the drawing was his—yet the notebook was his. Hauptmann gave no explanation.

The prosecution continued to damage Hauptmann's previous testimony. During a long question-and-answer exchange, Hauptmann admitted to telling several lies and withholding information from the police. For example, he had falsely told the police that he was hoarding twenty-dollar ransom bills to guard against the effects of money inflation (a rise in prices of things like food, clothing, and

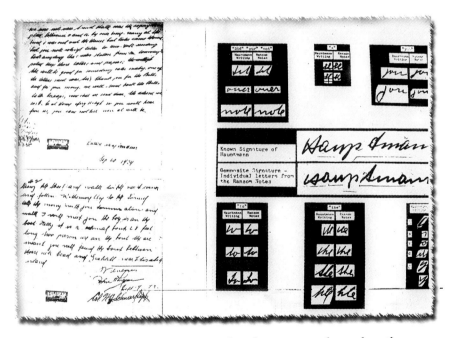

The state's handwriting experts produced many examples such as these of Hauptmann's writing. The prosecution wanted to prove that Hauptmann had written the ransom notes.

shelter). And, he had told police, after they had found the first chunk of ransom money, that that was all he had. Yet the police found more ransom money.

As the prosecution continued to hammer away at Hauptmann, more lies surfaced. Hauptmann had told some about Fisch. Originally, he had said that he had met Fisch in the Bronx in May 1932. Now he told the jury that a friend had introduced the two men in March or April of 1932. Fisch had died penniless, or so Fisch's family had been led to believe, since Fisch had arrived in Germany without any money. But that was not true. Hauptmann admitted that he had withheld from Fisch's family that Fisch had actually died with a great deal of money, only it was in Hauptmann's possession. Hauptmann still stuck to his story that all the money found by the police belonged to Fisch.

Wilentz now turned the jury's attention to the wooden trim taken from the Hauptmanns' closet. This piece of wood had Dr. Condon's address and telephone number written on it in pencil. Previously, Hauptmann had admitted that he had written this information. But when Wilentz showed Hauptmann the trim board and asked him to identify it, Hauptmann refused, saying that he could not tell if the trim had come from his house or someone else's. Then he denied that he had written Condon's information on the trim.

When questioned further, Hauptmann continued to deny that he had written Dr. Condon's phone number and address on the trim. Further, he said, the handwriting did look like his, but he could not "remember putting them numbers on" and that he was "positively sure I wouldn't write anything in the inside of a closet."[9]

Hauptmann did admit that he had written the serial numbers of a five-hundred and a thousand-dollar bill on the back of the same closet, on the closet door. By getting this admission, Wilentz hoped that the jury would think Hauptmann had written the serial numbers and Condon's information.[10]

Wilentz continued firing questions at Hauptmann, now focusing on his financial situation. Some of Hauptmann's explanations were so unbelievable that spectators in the courtroom laughed.[11]

Hauptmann had not proved to be a good witness for his case. For example, during his testimony, his face seldom showed any emotion and his voice was high and complaining. According to a reporter for *Time* magazine who was covering the trial, "[Cross-examination] made Hauptmann squirm in his chair, hang his head, and blush. Observers thought he either looked like a very embarrassed man or a very guilty one."[12]

Anna Hauptmann. After Bruno Hauptmann left the witness stand, Anna Hauptmann was questioned next. She first spoke about her early years of married life. Then the defense questioned her about the time of the kidnapping and the next few years.

Anna Hauptmann's testimony about the three important dates supported her husband's which helped backed up his alibis. Here is what she testified: On the night of the kidnapping, at 7:00 P.M., Hauptmann had come to the bakery where she worked. The two stayed at the bakery until 9:30, then they went straight to their apartment. That took care of one critical date.

April 2, 1932, was the date of the ransom payment. During that evening, Anna Hauptmann said she, her husband, and their friend Hans Kloppenburg were at the Hauptmanns' apartment until at least midnight.

Under questioning, she next moved to the third critical date of November 26, 1932. That date was her husband's birthday. No, she testified, her husband had *not* gone to a movie on November 26, 1933, as the prosecution had said. Instead, the couple held a small party in their apartment with several friends that evening.

During cross-examination, Wilentz focused his questions on the shoebox that had supposedly contained Fisch's ransom money. Hauptmann had claimed that just before Fisch had left for Germany, Fisch had given him the ransom money in a shoebox. Hauptmann put this shoebox on the top shelf of the Hauptmanns' kitchen closet.

During a question-and-answer exchange with Wilentz, Anna Hauptmann explained that she opened and used the kitchen closet every day. However, she admitted that she never saw a shoebox on the top shelf. By her own admission

Found near the Lindbergh home, the ladder used in the kidnapping was made of three interlocking parts. The prosecution argued that since Hauptmann was a carpenter, he was capable of building the ladder.

in court, Anna Hauptmann's testimony cast serious doubt on Hauptmann's claim that the ransom money had been left with him by Fisch.

Poor Alibi Witnesses

The defense produced a number of alibi witnesses to testify that Bruno Hauptmann was elsewhere during the time of the kidnapping on March 1, 1932. Elvert Carlstrom testified that he was at the Bronx bakery where Anna Hauptmann worked at 8:30 P.M. on March 1, 1932. Carlstrom claimed that he had seen Bruno Hauptmann at the bakery at this time. But when Wilentz cross-examined Carlstrom, the witness could not describe Hauptmann. Nor could Carlstrom describe any of the four or five other customers who were also there at that time. He also could not account for his time for the rest of the evening. There was more—Wilentz had found out that Carlstrom was a thief and former bootlegger, and had a history of severe mental health problems. Wilentz presented all this information to the jury during his cross-examination of Carlstrom.

The next alibi witness was Louis Kiss. Like Carlstrom, he claimed to have been at the same bakery on the evening of March 1, 1932. He said he had seen Hauptmann come into the bakery along with a police dog. Wilentz got Kiss to admit that he was a bootlegger, which made him a poor witness lacking in credibility.

August Van Henke owned a Manhattan restaurant. He testified that he had seen Hauptmann on the evening of March 1, 1932, at a gas station near the bakery where Anna

Hauptmann worked. Hauptmann, said the witness, had a police dog and Van Henke went over to talk with him about the dog. During his cross-examination, Wilentz soon discredited Van Henke. Van Henke admitted his restaurant had been a speakeasy and that he had used various names to avoid trouble with the law.

Another alibi witness was Lou Harding, a ditchdigger. According to Harding, on the morning of March 1, 1932, a blue car stopped by him while he worked. The two men inside asked for directions to the Lindberghs' house. As Harding gave directions, he noticed a ladder and a brown box in the back seat. After the kidnapping, when Harding reported this information to the police, he was taken to the Lindberghs' home. There he identified the ladder as the same one he had seen in the blue car. However, like the previous alibi witnesses, Harding was not credible. He had been jailed twice for committing various serious crimes. Further, he could not describe the ladder and changed his mind repeatedly about its color, size, length, and how it had been designed and made.

Philip Moses, a cabdriver, testified that he had seen three men beside a stalled green car near St. Raymond's Cemetery on April 2, 1932. This was the date of the ransom money exchange. Moses drove the three men to another street, where they got into a gray car. At this point, Moses told the jury that he had done other jobs besides taxi driving such as plumbing, acting, and dancing. He started to impersonate Will Rogers, a famous comedian of the time. As people laughed, Judge Trenchard rapped his gavel for order. But Moses provided no useful information about the three men.

Reilly had other alibi witnesses take the stand, but few helped Hauptmann's case. Hauptmann was not pleased with the choice of witnesses for his defense and back in his cell, he asked defense lawyer Fisher, "Where are they getting these witnesses from? They're really hurting me."[13]

Credible Alibi Witnesses

Several alibi witnesses *were* credible. One was Benjamin Lupica, a student at Princeton University. At six o'clock on the evening of March 1, 1932, Lupica claimed to have seen a man and a ladder in a car near the Lindberghs' home. Upon direct examination, Lupica said that Hauptmann was *not* the man in the car. However, he admitted that the man had resembled Hauptmann.

Hauptmann's friend, Hans Kloppenburg, testified. He said that he regularly went to the Hauptmanns' apartment on the first Saturday of every month. And, yes, he had been at the Hauptmanns' apartment on Saturday, April 2, 1932. Kloppenburg described the evening's activities. He also testified that he had been at Fisch's farewell party, which the Hauptmanns had held in December 1933. However, upon cross-examination by Wilentz, Kloppenburg admitted that he had previously told Wilentz that he could not remember what day in April 1932, he had actually been to the Hauptmanns' apartment.

A few personal friends testified that they had attended Hauptmann's birthday celebration on November 26, 1933.

Expert Witnesses

Dr. Erastus Mead Hudson, a medical doctor, had a hobby—fingerprinting. Although an amateur, he had been scientifically trained in his hobby and had practiced it for fifteen years. By using his method, Hudson had produced hundreds of fingerprints taken from the kidnapper's ladder. None, he testified, were Hauptmann's.

Although Reilly had promised the press that he would have at least eight handwriting experts testify, only one,

On May 13, 1932, President Herbert Hoover directed that the FBI, under J. Edgar Hoover (pictured), serve as the clearinghouse and coordinating agency for all investigations into the Lindbergh kidnapping case conducted by federal agencies.

John Trendley, spoke on the witness stand. The others refused to testify for various reasons. John Trendley, a documents examiner from St. Louis, Missouri, testified that although some similarities in spelling and grammar existed between Hauptmann's writing and the ransom notes, Hauptmann did not write the ransom letters. Why? Trendley said that Hauptmann's writing was uniform and the letters cleanly formed, but this was not true in the ransom note writing. Also, Hauptmann's handwriting was similar to that of many German-Americans for whom English was a second language.

Other Witnesses

Charles J. Debisschop, from Waterbury, Connecticut, was a lumberjack with thirty years of experience with wood. He said that he often matched wood grains of wood boards for cabinetmakers. From a large bag, he produced examples of matching wood grains, but the wood came from different trees. He testified that rail sixteen on the ladder did not come from Hauptmann's attic.

During the trial, the defense tried to put forth alternative theories about who could have kidnapped the Lindbergh baby. One was that Isidor Fisch had been involved. Another was that some of the Lindbergh and Morrow servants had been involved in the crime. A third was a combination—Fisch and the Lindbergh/Morrow servants were to blame.

One defense witness who was supposed to support this third theory was Peter H. Somner. He claimed to have seen three people—a woman, Isidor Fisch, and an unidentified man—with a baby on a New York ferry on March 1, 1932, at about midnight. Somner testified that the woman was Violet Sharpe. Sharpe had been a maid in the Morrow household during the time of the kidnapping.

But on cross-examination, Somner admitted that he had testified in dozens of other trials—for a fee. This meant he was a professional witness and this greatly reduced his credibility. Somner's credibility dropped even more when he could not identify Violet Sharpe from a photograph.

To the press, Reilly continued to say that Fisch had been guilty of the crime. Yet, although the defense had asked a dozen witnesses to come to the trial to support this theory, they all ignored the court's orders and never came to the trial.

Summaries

After the defense had finished presenting its witnesses, each side gave its closing statement. Both were five hours long. During these speeches, each side makes final summaries of the facts and tries to discredit the other side's witnesses and evidence. Reilly told the jurors, "I believe this man [Hauptmann] is absolutely innocent of murder."[14] Now, after twenty-nine court sessions and 162 witnesses, hundreds of exhibits and pieces of evidence, it was up to eight men and four women to decide if they agreed with Reilly.

chapter six

THE DECISION

COURTROOM—On the morning of February 13, 1935, Judge Trenchard began instructing the jury. Before the jury members left to deliberate, he told them that they were responsible for arriving at a verdict of guilty or not guilty. If their verdict was guilty, they were to determine to what degree Bruno Hauptmann was guilty. To do this, the jury members were to evaluate the evidence and determine if the state had shown that the defendant was guilty beyond a reasonable doubt.

Instructions to the Jury

Judge Trenchard reviewed some of the critical testimony and evidence that had been presented in the case, such as the handwriting analysis, ransom money, and the ladder. He reminded the jury that the state's case was circumstantial. That meant no one had actually seen Hauptmann kidnap or murder Charlie Lindbergh. Finally, he told the jury, if the defendant was guilty of murder in the first degree then they could recommend either life imprisonment at hard labor or death. Judge Trenchard finished his instructions at 11:13 that morning.

The Jury Deliberates

At 11:21 A.M., the jury room was declared ready. In this small room, directly above Hauptmann's cell, the jury members deliberated the case. They took some of the evidence with them. After all the jurors filed in, the sheriff locked the door. No one was permitted to hear what was discussed in the jury room.

The jurors took an initial vote. All voted for guilty— seven said Hauptmann should die by electrocution and five

Deliberating As a Juror

There is no set procedure that jurors must follow when deliberating a case. Each jury decides how to hold discussions, settle differences of opinion, and vote. Many judges give jurors the following information before they begin to deliberate:

1. Jurors must discuss the evidence presented on all important issues before taking a vote on the verdict.

2. All jurors should express their opinion during the deliberations.

3. No jurors should be pressured into changing their votes in order to arrive at a verdict more quickly.

4. Each juror should weigh opposing views carefully.

5. Any jurors can change their vote if a discussion has changed their point of view.

said he should receive life imprisonment.[1] After this, the jury members began to discuss the case. At three o'clock, they asked for a magnifying glass. They used it to look more closely at the ransom notes and the handwriting on the closet door trim. Three hours later, a meal was brought to the jury members. By this time, thousands of people were standing outside the courthouse waiting to hear the verdict. Continuous shouts of "Kill Hauptmann!" filled the air.[2] At 7:45 that evening, Judge Trenchard sent a message to the jurors, telling them that they could not leave the courthouse until they reached a verdict.

The Verdict

After about eleven-and-a-half hours of deliberation, at 10:27 P.M., the courthouse bell began to toll. It was a custom in Flemington to ring the courthouse bell when a verdict was ready to be announced. Hearing the bell, the crowd outside, which had swelled to seven thousand, chanted "Kill Hauptmann! Kill Hauptmann!"[3]

At 10:30, the jury filed into the courtroom. Hauptmann, with his feet in chains and his right wrist handcuffed to a state trooper, was brought in. Next, Judge Trenchard entered the courtroom. He waved his hand at the jury, then ordered them and Hauptmann to rise. Hauptmann stood along with his guards and state troopers. The foreperson, or head of the jurors, was asked if the jury had found the defendant guilty or not guilty.

The foreperson read slowly from a piece of paper as his

hands shook. "Guilty. We find the defendant, Bruno Richard Hauptmann, guilty of murder in the first degree."[4]

Several messengers ran to the door, to give the news to the press. But before they could get out, Judge Trenchard ordered that the courtroom doors be shut and that no one could leave. The court clerk asked the jury if they all agreed to this verdict. Yes, said the jurors. So the vote was unanimous.

Judge Trenchard told the defendant to stand. He repeated the verdict of guilty of murder in the first degree. Then he told Hauptmann that he would die by electrocution some-time during the week of March 18, 1935. At this point, a

The Flemington courthouse was always packed during Hauptmann's trial. Hauptmann is seated near the lower right corner (white circle).

messenger opened a window and shouted, "Guilty—death!" The waiting crowd roared its approval.[5]

Reactions to the Verdict

At 10:50 P.M., Hauptmann was led out of the courtroom. Locked into his prison cell, he fell face down on his cot and began to cry. Meanwhile, Anna Hauptmann also cried while she sat in the courtroom. After a while, a policeman escorted her outside.

Reporters telephoned the Lindberghs' home and asked to talk to the Lindberghs. A spokesperson at the house reported that the couple would not comment on the case or verdict.

Inside the household, Betty Morrow (Anne Lindbergh's mother) was the first to hear the news. She told the others that Hauptmann was to die for his crime. The Lindberghs turned on a radio in the library to hear the news firsthand. They sat without speaking, listening to the newscaster who was outside the Hunterdon County Courthouse. With a "howling mob" in the background, the radio newscaster said, "You have now heard the verdict in the most famous trial in all history. Bruno Hauptmann now stands guilty of one of the foulest. . . . "[6] At this point, Anne Lindbergh asked her husband to turn off the radio, which he did.

Everyone went to the kitchen. Colonel Lindbergh talked about his view on the case. "There is no doubt that Hauptmann did the thing. My one dread all these years has been that they would get hold of someone as a victim about whom I wasn't sure. I am sure about this—quite sure."[7] He then went through the case point by point, analyzing the witnesses and evidence.

Other reporters drove to John Condon's home in the Bronx to see if he would make a statement. Dr. Condon would not speak with the press. His wife, though, spoke for her husband, saying that they had heard the verdict and would not make any statements.

Some people did speak their views on the verdict. One was Eleanor Roosevelt (1884–1962), wife of President Franklin D. Roosevelt. Roosevelt was a social activist, author, and lecturer. Later she became an American representative to the United Nations. She disagreed with the death sentence because the evidence against Hauptmann had been mostly circumstantial. She explained to reporters, "The entire trial left me with a question in my mind. While I have no sympathy for Hauptmann, I can't help wondering what would happen if it were an innocent person on trial."[8]

The New York Times, a widely read American newspaper, reacted to Hauptmann's verdict as follows:

> We do not yet know exactly what happened on that tragic night at Hopewell. Nothing but a confession or the turning up of new evidence can throw further light upon a mystery which has all along been one of the most puzzling in criminal annals.[9]

But many people agreed with the *Daily News*, another large New York newspaper, which applauded the jury's verdict.

> [This verdict] will put a crimp in the snatch racket [kidnapping] from which it won't recover for a long time. The poor

little baby didn't die in vain. Everybody in this country who has children can feel a little safer today than yesterday.[10]

The Prisoner

Bruno Richard Hauptmann became Prisoner No. 17,400 in the New Jersey State Prison in Trenton. He occupied Cell 9—a nearly empty ten-by-eight-foot cell—in death row, an area for those sentenced to die for their crimes. Hauptmann's cell was only eight feet away from the electric chair. According to his sentencing, he would take that short walk during the week of March 18, 1935.

chapter seven

WHERE DO WE STAND TODAY?

TRENTON PRISON— Bruno Hauptmann's lawyers continued their legal fight. For over a year, they filed various appeals. An appeal is a legal request to review a case that has already gone through trial. In the end, the verdict of guilty of first-degree murder remained.

Appeals

Bruno Hauptmann's case had not completely closed. The Hauptmanns replaced Edward Reilly with Lloyd Fisher, who became Hauptmann's chief lawyer. On May 10, 1935, Fisher filed for a new trial, citing various reasons for reversal of Hauptmann's conviction. Reasons included extensive pretrial publicity, the circus-like atmosphere in the courtroom, Lindbergh's daily presence at the trial as prejudicial, and the fact that Judge Trenchard's instructions to the jury were biased toward the state. For these reasons, Hauptmann's new lawyer contended that he had been denied a fair trial under the Fourteenth Amendment of the United States Constitution. A month later, Fisher and

David T. Wilentz, the state's chief prosecutor, presented their sides to the New Jersey's Court of Errors and Appeals. Since only legal points were presented, no jury, witnesses, or spectators were allowed in the courtroom. The Hauptmanns could not attend. On October 9, 1935, in a forty-five-page report, the fourteen judges voted unanimously to uphold Hauptmann's conviction of guilty of first-degree murder.

Meanwhile, Anna Hauptmann did not remain idle. Appeals were costly. So she began to hold fund-raising rallies on behalf of her husband. She targeted the German-American communities in New Jersey and New York. Several of these rallies successfully raised money for Hauptmann's appeals.

Lloyd Fisher next appealed to the United States Supreme Court for a retrial. This court is the highest in the United States. But on December 9, 1935, the Supreme Court refused to review the constitutionality of Hauptmann's case. Judge Trenchard set Hauptmann's execution for January 17, 1936.

Since the highest court in the land had refused to even consider Hauptmann's case, Fisher tried one last option to ask that Hauptmann's life be spared. He filed a final appeal with the New Jersey Court of Pardons on December 23, 1935. Governor Harold Hoffmann was a member of the New Jersey Court of Pardons. This court met on January 11, 1936. Fisher and Wilentz again presented their cases to a panel. In addition to Governor Hoffman, the panel members also included five judges and two laypersons. The

Hauptmanns were not allowed to attend. Fisher had several witnesses testify, then asked the court to spare Hauptmann's life. Within a few hours, the panel reached its decision. The members voted seven to one to uphold Hauptmann's death sentence. The only person who did not agree was Governor Hoffman.

Governor Hoffman Investigates

Governor Hoffman disagreed because he had doubts that one man could have committed the crime. He felt that Hauptmann had been "tried and convicted in the newspapers."[1] Afterward, he visited Hauptmann in his jail cell. Then, only days before the execution, Governor Hoffman announced that he was giving Hauptmann a thirty-day grace period and that he would conduct his own investigation of the crime.

Across the country, people were outraged over his actions because it appeared as if Hoffman was trying to second-guess Judge Trenchard, the jury, the appeals court, and the court of pardons.[2] Newspapers nationwide expressed anger over Governor Hoffman's actions. Some people wanted Hoffman impeached, or removed from office. Hoffman said he only wanted to see justice done.[3]

Hoffman assembled a team to investigate Hauptmann's case. His main investigator was Ellis Parker, a detective. But with time slipping by quickly, Hoffman and his team did not uncover anything useful for Hauptmann's case. Instead, a new twist developed in the Lindbergh baby kidnapping case.

A Bizarre Confession

On March 27, 1936, the eight members of the New Jersey Court of Pardons received a typewritten, twenty-five-page confession in the mail. It was signed by Paul H. Wendel. In the confession, Wendel said he had kidnapped and killed the Lindbergh baby. In addition to taking the baby, he wrote, he was Cemetery John and had taken the ransom money from John Condon. Wendel had supposedly just told Ellis Parker of his crimes, which is why he had written a confession.

Was Wendel telling the truth? The New Jersey State Police investigated Wendel's background and discovered that he had been a successful lawyer. But in 1920 he had committed a crime, spent nine months in jail, and had been disbarred, which meant he could no longer practice law. After leaving jail, he committed more crimes—writing bad checks and stealing—and also spent some time in a New Jersey insane asylum, or institution for the mentally ill, before disappearing. No one, including his family, could find him. Meanwhile, the state was waiting to arrest Wendel for theft and writing bad checks.

Parker turned Wendel over to the New Jersey State Police for his unpunished crimes. Attorney General David T. Wilentz of New Jersey asked Wendel if his confession was true.

No, it was not, said Wendel. After admitting that he had been forced to confess his supposed crime to Ellis Parker, he showed Wilentz an assortment of bruises and welts on his legs. He claimed that Ellis Parker, along with Parker's son and several other men, had kidnapped him and forced him to confess to the kidnapping and murder of the Lindbergh baby.

Wendel's bizarre story proved to be true. Parker had written the twenty-five page confession. He had forced Wendel to sign it by keeping him a prisoner in a mental institution for three weeks, beating him regularly, and threatening to keep him there permanently unless he signed the confession. Under a new 1934 federal kidnapping law, Parker, his son, and the other men were sentenced to prison for kidnapping Wendel.

Final Days

On March 30, the court of pardons met to hear Hauptmann's final request that his life be spared. Fisher and Wilentz presented their cases. At 4:00 P.M., the eight-member panel left the courtroom to discuss Hauptmann's request. The decision was announced within an hour: Hauptmann was to die in the electric chair on April 3, 1936.

Dozens of people were invited to watch Hauptmann's execution. They included policemen, members of the media, politicians, medical doctors, and Hauptmann's defense lawyers. By early evening, thousands of reporters and spectators had gathered outside the prison gates. Hundreds of police and state troopers stood ready in case the crowd became unruly.

Hauptmann had written a final statement, which was given to Fisher when he entered Hauptmann's cell to say good-bye. In the letter, Hauptmann once again said he was innocent of the crime. Fisher pleaded, "Richard, tell me something that will save your life."

"There isn't anything I can say," Hauptmann replied.[4]

Hauptmann was electrocuted at 8:47 P.M. The crowd quickly broke up once the prisoner's death was announced. The next day, headlines carried the news of Hauptmann's death. One headline summed up Hauptmann's final moments: "Hauptmann Dies in Chair. Remains Silent Until End."[5] Hauptmann's body was cremated.

Federal Kidnapping Law

As a result of the Lindbergh baby's kidnapping, a new federal law was passed in 1934, commonly called the

Bruno Richard Hauptmann was executed in the electric chair on April 3, 1936, over four years after Charlie Lindbergh was kidnapped.

Lindbergh Act. This was the first federal kidnapping law in the United States. And it was the law under which Ellis Parker and his cohorts were tried and convicted of the kidnapping of Paul H. Wendel.

In 1980, the federal government passed the Parental Kidnapping Prevention Act. In 1982 and 1984, the federal government increased its role in parental kidnapping cases and other forms of child disappearance by passing the Missing Children's Act and the Missing Children's Assistance Act.

These laws provide information and resources to parents and state and local governments to help local children. These laws, for the first time, made the FBI available as a resource of information. In 1984 the federal government established a national clearinghouse for gathering information about missing children and established a toll-free hotline for reporting abductions and gathering information about missing children.

Cameras Banned in Courtrooms

At one point during Hauptmann's trial, a large motion picture camera and a microphone had been set up in the courtroom. The camera was fixed on the witness stand. Thanks to this filming, moviegoers could see the actual trial proceedings. The judge, lawyers, and police had no knowledge that the trial was being filmed.

But when David Wilentz, the New Jersey attorney general, found out about the filming, he informed Judge Trenchard. The judge immediately ordered all motion picture equipment out of the courtroom for the remainder of the trial. He also said that he would not take legal action against the filmmakers as long as the newsreels were not shown during the time the case was being tried. Based on this incident and because motion pictures can sway emotions during a trial, cameras have been banned from most American trials for over six decades.

Unfair Trial?

Over the years, the *Hauptmann* case has sparked much controversy. One debated issue is whether Hauptmann received a fair trial. Some experts such as Jim Fisher believe that Hauptmann's trial *was* fair. Fisher is an expert on the Hauptmann case and was a former FBI agent and professor of criminal justice at Edinboro University in Edinboro, Pennsylvania. He wrote in his book, *The Lindbergh Case,*

> Hauptmann received as fair a trial as could be expected under the circumstances. The trial judge was unbiased, experienced, and competent, and the jury was made up of intelligent and rational people with a lot of common sense. Moreover, Hauptmann took advantage of a full range of appeals.[6]

Other experts disagree. "Few today deny that the trial [Hauptmann's] was unfair—not only by current standards, but by the far less rigorous standards of the 1930s," said Alan M. Dershowitz, a lawyer and law professor.[7]

Experts cite various reasons why the trial was unfair. Some have said that evidence presented at the trial may have been ignored, tampered with, or even made up. For example, some witnesses may have been paid to change their testimony. By contrast, other experts say that no evidence was made up or ignored. Controversy over the major evidence— such as the ladder, ransom notes, and John F. Condon's address and telephone number written in Hauptmann's closet—has continued to rage throughout the years.

Another point of contention is that Hauptmann's ability to speak and understand English was limited. His native language was German. Although he spoke "halting" English with a heavy accent, he was not asked if he wanted a translator during the trial.[8] Edward J. Reilly, Hauptmann's chief lawyer during the trial, was a well-known criminal attorney with many court wins to his credit. Yet some experts have said that he did a poor job of representing Hauptmann and that he may have been drunk during much of the trial. Further, there was a conflict of interest. The publishers of a large newspaper, the *New York Journal*, made a deal with the Hauptmanns: they would hire and pay Edward Reilly to defend Hauptmann if Anna Hauptmann gave the newspaper exclusive (the only) rights to her story. The Hauptmanns agreed and Reilly got paid in full for his legal work before the trial began. Since he had been prepaid, Reilly may not have worked very hard for Hauptmann during the trial. Also, Reilly kept a photo of his hero Charles Lindbergh on his desk throughout the trial and at one point told an FBI agent that "he knew Hauptmann was guilty, didn't like him, and was anxious to see him get the chair."[9]

Experts point to other factors that made for an unfair trial. The jury lived under conditions that would not be allowed today. They regularly heard people discussing the case during their meals, which were served three times a day at the Union Hotel, across the street from the Hunterdon County Courthouse. Newspaper and radio journalists regularly ate at the hotel and many discussed their negative views of the case, describing the defendant as "Hauptmann the baby-killer."[10] The jury walked between the hotel and courthouse three or four times a day. Each time, they saw a constant crowd of vendors, reporters, and spectators, many shouting "Burn Hauptmann" or chanting that Hauptmann was one day closer to the electric chair.[11]

During the five-week trial, the press "went wild, muddying things up considerably" from the time of the kidnapping to Hauptmann's execution.[12] After the trial, *Editor and Publisher* magazine criticized the media for creating a circuslike atmosphere during Hauptmann's trial. The lawyers for each side may have violated, or broken, legal standards. Here are some examples: During the trial, both David Wilentz and Edward Reilly made frequent public statements to the press or radio about the case. These actions may be against the American Lawyers' Canon of Professional Ethics. Judge Trenchard did not discipline the lawyers for talking to the press. The judge also did not discipline the press during the trial. Instead, reporters were allowed to taunt and poke Hauptmann during the trial.

Continuing Controversy

When Bruno Richard Hauptmann was executed in 1936, many people said that he was guilty of kidnapping and murdering the Lindbergh baby. Yet, over the years, doubt has crept in and some people's attitudes have shifted. Why the change?

One reason for the doubt about Hauptmann's guilt is that the public's attitude toward Colonel Charles Lindbergh may have changed. After Hauptmann was arrested, the Lindberghs began receiving a lot of hate mail. Some were death threats against Jon, their second son. Lindbergh recalled that during that time "life for my family became so difficult, disagreeable, and dangerous that I decided to take up residence abroad until such time as we could live in our own country with reasonable assurance."[13] Because of the continued threats on Jon's life, the Lindberghs left the United States on December 22, 1935, and moved to England.[14] The public had mixed reactions to the hero and his family leaving America. Some called Colonel Lindbergh a quitter.[15]

Colonel Lindbergh sparked further controversy among Americans during the time he lived in Europe when he was invited to inspect the German air force. He did so several times. By this time, the world was on the brink of World War II (1939–1945) and Germany was one of the countries that the United States would fight against during the war. At this time, Adolf Hitler was the German dictator and leader of the German National Socialist (Nazi) party, which preached and followed a type of fascism. Fascism is a dictatorship with government control of the economy and suppression of all opposition. Lindbergh openly praised Adolph Hitler and his government.

After returning to the United States in 1939 before World War II broke out, the colonel stirred further debate. He began to make a series of national radio speeches urging America to stay out of the war. The United States entered the war in 1941.

All these actions made some Americans think less of their former hero; he seemed "tainted with fascism."[16] As a result, some people began to think Lindbergh was somehow to blame for Hauptmann's execution.[17] Perhaps he had covered up important information or maybe he had been mistaken about hearing Hauptmann as Cemetery John.

Concerned about the safety of their son Jon, Anne and Charles Lindbergh moved their family to England on December 22, 1935.

Anna Hauptmann also sustained doubt in some people's mind about the supposed guilt of her husband. She spent much of her life trying to show that her husband was innocent. "I know the truth, and I fight for the truth," she told reporters in 1985.[18] She tried in 1981 and again in 1986 to have the case reopened and to clear her husband's name. Later, she asked the governor of New Jersey to conduct a new investigation. He refused. She died at the age of ninety-five on October 10, 1994, still insisting that her husband was innocent.

Over the years, people have developed their own theories about who kidnapped and killed the Lindbergh baby—and whether Hauptmann was guilty or innocent. Many articles, books, plays, and movies on Hauptmann's trial have been created. Each has its own viewpoint and conclusions.

Although the trial of the century came to a close in 1936, people still debate whether or not Bruno Richard Hauptmann was guilty—and if so, what was he guilty of? Hauptmann himself predicted the aftermath of his trial, when shortly before his death he told Governor Harold Hoffman of New Jersey, "They think when I die, the case will die. They think it will be like a book I close. But the book, it will never close."[19]

Questions for Discussion

1. In your opinion, why has the verdict in Bruno Richard Hauptmann's case remained so famous for so long?

2. Why do you think Colonel Lindbergh was allowed to run the kidnapping investigation up to the point of the discovery of the dead child?

3. Did the police have enough probable cause to arrest Hauptmann? Why or why not? Explain in your own words.

4. Defendants do not have to testify during their trial. Would it have been a good idea that Hauptmann testified? Why or why not?

5. Ann Morrow Lindbergh's testimony was not crucial to the trial. If you were the prosecutor, would you have had Mrs. Lindbergh testify? Why or why not?

6. During the trial, some of the defense's witnesses directly contradicted the prosecution's witnesses. Why do you think witnesses can present such different versions of what they saw or heard?

7. Hauptmann's trial took five weeks. Both sides presented a mass of evidence and many witnesses. The jury took over eleven hours to deliberate this case. Was this enough time for them to discuss all the important testimony and evidence presented in the trial? Explain your answer.

8. On the basis of the information presented in this book, do you think Hauptmann was guilty or innocent of the charges against him? Why or why not?

9. Did Colonel Lindbergh make an accurate identification of Hauptmann's voice as Cemetery John? Why or why not?

10. Throughout Hauptmann's trial, Colonel Lindbergh openly wore a gun in a shoulder holster. However, when he testified, he was unarmed. Why do you think Colonel Lindbergh wore a gun to Hauptmann's trial? Why do you think Lindbergh was unarmed when he gave his testimony?

11. Compared to newspapers, what are the advantages radio and television offered to people who followed the trial?

12. Why were so many guards were stationed near Hauptmann while he testified? What message, if any, do you think this sent to the jury?

Chapter Notes

Chapter 1. Stolen Baby

1. Dorothy Herrmann, *Anne Morrow Lindbergh: A Gift for Life* (New York: Ticknor & Fields, 1992), p. 91.

2. Gregory Ahlgren and Stephen Monier, *Crime of the Century: The Lindbergh Kidnapping Hoax* (Boston, Mass.: Branden Books, 1993), p. 15.

Chapter 2. America in the 1930s

1. Marc McCutcheon, *Everyday Life from Prohibition through World War II* (Cincinnati, Ohio: Writer's Digest Books, 1995), p. 61.

2. Ibid., p. 62.

3. Paula S. Fass, *Kidnapped: Child Abduction in America* (New York: Oxford University Press, 1997), p. 107.

4. Michael E. Parrish, *Anxious Decades: America in Prosperity and Depression, 1920-1941* (New York: W.W. Norton & Company, 1992), p. 179.

5. Joyce Milton, *Loss of Eden: A Biography of Charles and Anne Morrow Lindbergh* (New York: HarperCollins Publishers, 1993), p. 159.

6. Ibid., p. 162.

7. Charles A. Lindbergh, *Autobiography of Values* (New York: Harcourt, Brace Jovanovich, 1992), p. 139.

Chapter 3. The Road to Court

1. Charles A. Lindbergh, *Autobiography of Values* (New York: Harcourt, Brace Jovanovich, 1992), p. 139.

2. Ibid.

3. Ibid.

4. Melanie Weaver, "Ransom Notes, Responses, and Other Communications," *The Lindbergh Kidnapping*, © 1998

<http://www.law.umkc.edu/faculty/projects/trials/lindbergh/ RANSOM.htm> (February 11, 1999).

5. A. Scott Berg, *Lindbergh* (New York: G. P. Putnam's Sons, 1998), p. 245.

6. Anne Morrow Lindbergh, *Hour of Gold, Hour of Lead: Diaries and Letters 1929–1932* (New York: Harcourt Brace Jovanovich, 1973), p. 229.

7. Weaver, <http://www.law.umkc.edu/faculty/projects/trials/ lindbergh/RANSOM.htm>.

8. Russell Aiuto, "Lindbergh," © 1998 <http://www. crimelibrary.com/lindbergh/lindmain.htm/> (October 29, 1999).

9. Charles Lindbergh, p. 140.

10. Joyce Milton, *Loss of Eden: A Biography of Charles and Anne Morrow Lindbergh* (New York: HarperCollins Publishers, 1993), p. 246.

11. Berg, p. 267.

12. Hunterdon County Democrat, "The Lindbergh Baby Kidnapping Trial," © 1998 <http://lindberghtrial.com/> (June 3, 1998).

13. FBI Home Page, "The Lindbergh Case," © 1998 <http:// www.fbi.gov/famcases/hauptmann.html> (November 13, 1998).

14. Aiuto, <http://www.crimelibrary.com/lindbergh/ lindmain.htm/> (October 7, 1999).

15. Jim Fisher, *The Lindbergh Case* (New Brunswick, N.J.: Rutgers University Press, 1987), p. 188.

16. Milton, p. 293.

17. Ibid., p. 271.

18. Hunterdon County Democrat, "The Lindbergh Trial," © 1998 <http://www.lindberghtrial.com/> (June 3, 1998).

19. Ibid.

Chapter 4. The Case for New Jersey

1. "Trial Excerpts," University of Missouri, © 1998 <http:// www.law.umkc.edu/faculty/projects/trials/lindbergh/wilenz.htm> (February 11, 1999).

2. Joyce Milton, *Loss of Eden: A Biography of Charles and Anne Morrow Lindbergh* (New York: HarperCollins Publishers, 1993), p. 305.

3. George Waller, *Kidnap: The Story of the Lindbergh Case* (New York: The Dial Press, 1961), p. 286.

4. Barry Denenberg, *An American Hero: The True Story of Charles A. Lindbergh* (New York: Scholastic, Inc., 1996), p. 161.

5. Noel Behn, *Lindbergh: The Crime* (New York: The Atlantic Monthly Press, 1994), p. 250.

6. A. Scott Berg, *Lindbergh* (New York: G. P. Putnam's Sons, 1998), p. 315.

7. Anne Morrow Lindbergh, *Locked Rooms and Open Doors: Diaries and Letters of Anne Morrow Lindbergh, 1933–1935* (New York: Harcourt Brace Jovanovich, 1974), p. 235.

8. Waller, pp. 313–314.

9. Berg, p. 316.

10. Jim Fisher, *The Lindbergh Case* (New Brunswick, N.J.: Rutgers University Press, 1987), p. 289.

11. Waller, p. 319.

12. Ibid., p. 329.

13. Ludovic Kennedy, *The Airman and the Carpenter* (New York: Viking Press, 1985), p. 289.

14. Waller, p. 345.

15. Fisher, p. 304.

16. Ibid., p. 305.

17. FBI, "Bruno Richard Hauptmann," © 1998 <http://www.fbi.gov/famcases/hauptmans.html> (November 13, 1998).

18. Behn, p. 255.

19. Berg, p. 323.

Chapter 5. The Case for Bruno Hauptmann

1. Hunterdon County Democrat, "The Lindbergh Case," © 1998 <http://www.lindberghtrial.com/> (June 3, 1998).

2. "Crime: New Jersey v. Hauptmann," *Time*, January 30, 1995, p. 21.

3. Ibid.

4. Jim Fisher, *The Lindbergh Case* (New Brunswick, N.J.: Rutgers University Press, 1987), pp. 325–326.

5. Ibid.

6. Ibid., p. 325.

7. A. Scott Berg, *Lindbergh* (New York: G. P. Putnam's Sons, 1998), p. 324.

8. Fisher, pp. 325–326.

9. Berg, p. 326.

10. Fisher, p. 327.

11. Berg, p. 327.

12. "Crime: New Jersey v. Hauptmann," p. 21.

13. Fisher, p. 345.

14. Joyce Milton, *Loss of Eden: A Biography of Charles and Anne Morrow Lindbergh* (New York: HarperCollins Publishers, 1993), p. 326.

Chapter 6. The Decision

1 Joyce Milton, *Loss of Eden: A Biography of Charles and Anne Morrow Lindbergh* (New York: HarperCollins Publishers, 1993),p. 326.

2. Barry Denenberg, *An American Hero: The True Story of Charles A. Lindbergh* (New York: Scholastic, Inc., 1996), p. 169.

3. A. Scott Berg, *Lindbergh* (New York: G. P. Putnam's Sons, 1998), p. 332.

4. Jim Fisher, *The Lindbergh Case* (New Brunswick, N.J.: Rutgers University Press, 1987), p. 373.

5. Edward Oxford, "The Other Trial of the Century," *American History*, July 1995, p. 68.

6. Russell Aiuto, "Lindbergh," © 1998 <http://www.crimelibrary.com/lindbergh/lindmain.htm/> (October 27, 1999).

7. Berg, p. 333.

8. George Waller, *Kidnap: The Story of the Lindbergh Case* (New York: The Dial Press, 1961), p. 497.

9. Oxford, p. 69.

10. Waller, p. 498.

Chapter 7. Where Do We Stand Today?

1. Edward Oxford, "The Other Trial of the Century," *American History*, July 1995, p. 69.

2. Jim Fisher, *The Lindbergh Case* (New Brunswick, N.J.: Rutgers University Press, 1987), p. 397.

3. Russell Aiuto, "Lindbergh," © 1998 <http://www.crimelibrary.com/lindbergh/lindmain.htm/> (October 26, 1999).

4. Oxford, p. 69.

5. A. Scott Berg, *Lindbergh* (New York: G. P. Putnam's Sons, 1998), p. 329.

6. Fisher, p. 5.

7. Berg, p. 334.

8. Gregory Ahlgren and Stephen Monier, *Crime of the Century: The Lindbergh Kidnapping Hoax* (Boston, Mass.: Branden Books, 1993), p. 148.

9. Ibid., p. 304.

10. Anthony Scaduto, *Scapegoat: The Lonesome Death of Bruno Richard Hauptmann* (New York: G.P. Putnam's Sons, 1976), p. 119.

11. Ibid.

12. "The Lindbergh Case," *Hunterdon County Democrat*, © 1998, <http://www.lindberghtrial.com/> (June 3, 1998).

13. Charles A. Lindbergh, *Autobiography of Values* (New York: Harcourt, Brace Jovanovich, 1992), p. 18.

14. Ahlgren and Monier, p. 194.

15. George Waller, *Kidnap: The Story of the Lindbergh Case* (New York: The Dial Press, 1961), p. 225.

16. Russell Aiuto, "Lindbergh," © 1998 <http://www.crimelibrary.com/lindbergh/lindmain.htm/> (October 26, 1999).

17. Ibid.

18. "Anna Hauptmann; Lindbergh Kidnapping's Final Victim," *U.S. News & World Report*, November 4, 1985, p. 11.

19. Scaduto, p. 484.

Glossary

abduction—Kidnapping of an adult or child.

alibi—A reason why a defendant could not have done what he or she is accused of doing. This is usually a statement by a witness that the defendant was someplace else at the time of the crime.

amendment—New provisions to the Constitution, or changes to a particular portion of the Constitution.

appeal—Asking a court with a greater authority to review the decision of a lower court.

Bill of Rights—The first ten amendments to the United States Constitution, which protect the rights of individuals. The Bill of Rights gives Americans many freedoms and protections such as freedom of religions, speech, and the press.

burden of proof—The amount of evidence required in a case in order for the jury to find in favor of the person bringing the lawsuit. The more serious the consequences of the case, the greater the amount of proof required.

closing arguments—At the end of the testimony, the lawyers for each side sum up what they believe the jury's verdict should be.

criminal case—A legal action started by a state or federal prosecutor in the name of the state or United States against a person accused of committing a crime and asking for a punishment.

cross-examination—Questioning of a witness by the lawyer who did not call the witness.

cyanide—A strong poison.

defendant—A person in a trial who is accused of a crime.

defense lawyer—A lawyer who acts of behalf of a person who is accused of a crime.

deliberations—A jury's discussion and evaluation of the evidence presented in a trial.

evidence—Any statement or object presented in a court case as a proof of fact.

expert witness—A person with specialized knowledge or experience in some area who testifies as a recognized authority.

extradition—The surrender of an alleged criminal by one state to another having the jurisdiction, or legal authority, to try the charge.

fascism—A dictatorship with government control of the economy and suppression of all opposition.

foreperson—Chair on a jury; the person who leads or organizes the discussion of a jury and is responsible for trying to keep order.

grand jury—A jury that investigates criminal complaints and decides if someone should be formally charged with committing a crime.

Great Depression—On October 29, 1929, the New York Stock Exchange, the largest in the world, crashed. This led to an American economic depression, called the

Great Depression. It grew into a worldwide economic depression by the early 1930s.

immigrant—A person who has left his or her homeland and comes to live permanently in another country.

indictment—A formal written accusation prepared for a court by a grand jury. It outlines what crime or crimes are believed to have been committed and names the person or persons who probably committed those crimes.

jury—A group of people who have sworn to decide the facts in a court case and to reach a fair verdict or decision.

lineup—A line of people, including the suspect, arranged by the police for identification by witnesses.

mistrial—A trial that has no legal effect by reason of some error or serious prejudicial misconduct.

moonshining—The illegal making of homemade whiskey.

Nazi—Someone who who supports any government or shares the political beliefs like that developed by dictator Adolf Hitler in German in the 1920s.

opening statements—The presentation made by the lawyers on each side of the case at the start of a trial. During opening statements, the issues and facts that will be presented are outlined. The purpose of the opening statements is to give the jury an overview of the case, to help them understand the evidence they will hear.

Prohibition—The period in United States history when the manufacture and sale of alcoholic beverages was illegal.

prosecutor—Government official authorized to accuse and

prosecute (bring to trial) someone who is believed to have committed a crime. Prosecutors are known by various names in different parts of the United States: district attorney, state's attorney, and people's attorney.

ransom note—A letter from kidnappers demanding something in exchange for return of the kidnapped person.

sentence—In criminal cases, the decision by a jury or judge as to what punishment is appropriate for a convicted defendant.

testimony—Evidence given after taking an oath in court to tell the truth; questions answered under oath concerning what one knows about a case being heard in court.

United States Constitution—This document, which went into effect in 1787, covers the basic laws and principles by which America is governed.

verdict—The decision that a jury or judge makes after hearing and considering all of the evidence and testimony in a case.

witness—Someone who has seen or heard something pertaining to a court case; someone who provides evidence about something in a court of law.

Further Reading

Ahlgren, Gregory, and Stephen Monier. *Crime of the Century: The Lindbergh Kidnapping Hoax.* Boston: Branden Publishing Company, Inc., 1993.

Behn, Noel. *Lindbergh: The Crime.* New York: The Atlantic Monthly Press, 1994.

Berg, A. Scott. *Lindbergh.* New York: G. P. Putnam's Sons, 1998.

Denenberg, Barry. *An American Hero: The True Story of Charles A. Lindbergh.* New York: Scholastic, Inc., 1996.

Giblin, James C. *Charles A. Lindbergh: A Human Hero.* Boston: Houghton Mifflin Company, 1997.

Internet Addresses

Russell Aiuto, "Lindbergh: The Theft of the Eaglet," © 1998 <http://www.crimelibrary.com/lindbergh/lindmain.htm>

Melanie Weaver, Rebecca McGinley, and Gregory Egan, "Famous American Trials: The Trial of Bruno Richard Hauptmann," The University of Missouri Law School, <http://www.law.umkc.edu/faculty/projects/ftrials/lindbergh/lindb.htm>

The Lindbergh Case <http://www.lindberghtrial.com/html/bruno1a.htm>

Index